TODAY'S
GOURMET II

KQED, INC. • SAN FRANCISCO

TODAY'S GOURMET II

Light and Healthy Cooking for the '90s

JACQUES PEPIN

We gratefully acknowledge the following sponsors of the public television series "TODAY'S GOURMET WITH JACQUES PEPIN"

Managing Editor: Zipporah Collins

Book Designer: Laura Lamar

Photographer: Penina

Photography Coordinator: Susie Heller

Food / Photography Stylist: Bernie Schimbke

Photography Chef: Carl Abbott

Assistant to Jacques Pépin: Norma Galehouse

Cover Portrait: Larry Dyer

Credits Page Portrait: Bill Lyle

Illustrations: Jacques Pépin

Project Director: Bradford C. Stauffer

Props provided by: Botticelli, Crate & Barrel, Limoges, Macy's, Pierre Deux, Pottery Barn, Tag, Williams-Sonoma.

Library of Congress Cataloging-in-Publication Data
Pépin, Jacques.
    Today's Gourmet II : light and healthy cooking for the '90s / Jacques Pépin
       p. cm.
    Based on the author/chef's Public Television series.
    Includes index.
    ISBN 0-912333-16-2 : $14.95
    1. Cookery. 2. Today's gourmet (Television program).
I. Title. II. Title: Today's gourmet two. III. Title: Today's gourmet 2.
TX714.P46 1992
641.5—dc20   92–27810
                                                          CIP
Manufactured in the United States of America

CONTENTS

ACKNOWLEDGMENTS
page vi

INTRODUCTION
page vii

MENUS
page 1

FIRST COURSES
page 17

MAIN COURSES
page 71

ACCOMPANIMENTS
page 107

DESSERTS
page 127

MISCELLANEOUS
page 157

HEALTH NOTES
page 167

INDEX
page 171

ACKNOWLEDGMENTS

The production of "Today's Gourmet with Jacques Pépin" the television series, as well as *Today's Gourmet II* the cookbook, required a concerted effort on the part of many, many capable people. I would like to thank everyone involved with these projects for their support and hard work.

It is impossible to name every person associated with all the various facets of the television show, but I especially want to thank:

Marjorie Poore, vice-president in charge of television productions for KQED and project director for the series, for turning her confidence in me and her vision of the series into a marketable reality; *Peter Stein*, my executive producer, for confronting and resolving every problem with intelligence and humor; *Peggy Scott*, my producer, for amiably and ably overseeing every detail of the show; *Susie Heller*, my associate producer and dear friend, for her culinary insights, her enthusiasm, and, most of all, her honesty; *June Ouellette*, staff associate producer, for all her good work and support; *Katherine Russell*, my director, for quietly and capably guiding us through our hectic taping schedule; *Jolee Hoyt*, unit manager, for keeping us on budget; *Bernie Schimbke* and *Merilee Hague*, for their gifted prop work and food styling; *Claire Bechtel*, for her helpful nutritional consultations; and, of course, *Carl Abbott*, my great back kitchen supervisor, and his incredible staff, *Gwilym Fong, Mary Cramer, Josie Ingber, Travis Brady*, and *Mike Pleiss*.

For their help with the cookbook, I am grateful to:

Brad Stauffer, project director for the book, who coordinated our cross-country collaboration; *Zipporah Collins*, project managing editor, who polished our manuscript to produce a concise, well-organized book; *Laura Lamar*, project art director, who delivered a cover and interior design that pleased us all; *Penina*, who did the food photography; *Larry Dyer*, who took the cover portrait; *Bill Lyle*, who took the credits page photo; and finally, *Norma Galehouse*, my longtime assistant, who transformed my handwritten recipes and taped introductions into a manuscript.

INTRODUCTION

Today's *Gourmet II* is a continuation of the type of cuisine I introduced in the original television series and its companion cookbook. My common-sense approach to cooking—the way I cook at home on a regular basis—has been extremely well received, and I thank viewers for their enthusiastic response to *Today's Gourmet*, both the series and the book. ❦ It is not my intention to do dietetic cooking here, nor do I banish all butter, cream, and other types of fat from my recipes; rather, I use small amounts of these ingredients, adding them at the precise moment when they maximize flavor. Essentially, I advocate the use of quality ingredients and the value and healthfulness of organic products. ❦ In the "happy cooking" I do, I also want to teach you how to cook better and faster. You should have fun in the kitchen and then emerge from it with flavorful, wholesome, attractive dishes that can be served to both family and guests. Some of the recipes are simple, lending themselves more to family meals; others, containing costlier ingredients, are more elaborate, better suited to parties. ❦ All the recipes in the book reflect my style of life and my approach to cooking, suggesting how I incorporate cooking into the context of my family life, which includes countless gatherings. Food is the common denominator that brings people together in my house, and this way of life is represented in the recipes that follow.

INTRODUCTION TO TODAY'S GOURMET I

When I recall the food that we used to serve at Le Pavillon in New York when I first came to America thirty years ago, I realize how much cooking in general has changed and improved, especially in the last twenty years or so. ❦ I like to think that my cooking has changed a great deal, too. Through the years, I have tried to keep abreast of what's going on and have made adjustments in my cooking to accommodate changes brought about, for example, by the social upheavals of the sixties and seventies, spanning everything from women's liberation to organic gardening—one offshoot of a tremendous national concern about health. ❦ Paradoxically, the current preoccupation with health as it relates to food is not a new or revolutionary phenomenon.

Dating back as far as the ancient Greek poet and gastronome Archestratus and the Romans, and continuing through the cooking of the sixteenth, seventeenth, and eighteenth centuries, food has always been closely associated with health. In fact, most of the cookbooks prior to the nineteenth century were gastro-medical in nature, and there are early twentieth-century examples of these as well: A book by Dr. Edouard de Pomiane, published during World War II, dealt with healthful eating in times when food supplies are scarce. ❦ The trend today is a return to that basic notion of health encapsulated in Brillat-Savarin's aphorism "you are what you eat." The same idea was expressed later by Thomas Alva Edison, who said, "The doctor of the future will give no medicine, but will educate his patients in the care of the human frame, in diet, and in the cause and prevention of disease." ❦ The concerns of modern, well-educated eaters parallel those of modern, well-educated chefs and go beyond how food tastes and how it is presented. Today's astute food buyer wants produce that is not only fresh but also free of chemicals. The quality of the products in our diet directly affects the quality of our health and the health of our families. We have to stay in tune with nature; if the chickens we eat feed on grass and natural grains in an area free of pesticides and insecticides, their quality and the quality of the eggs they produce will improve substantially. ❦ Health concerns me greatly in *Today's Gourmet*. Although this is not intended to be a low-calorie, low-fat, low-sodium, or low-cholesterol book, the recipes here reflect how important I think it is to moderate our intake of these nutritional components. Keep in mind, however, that I am a cook, not a doctor. I am not a guru of macrobiotic food, insisting on the wholesomeness of grains and fiber, nor have I assumed the role of a nutritionist, advising people on what they should or should not eat. Eating, for me, has always meant enjoyment and sharing, never prohibitions. ❦ In these pages, I want to introduce you to a cuisine that demonstrates a rational approach to cooking. It is a sensitive and sensible way to cook, a cooking style that emphasizes aspects of health in a commonsense way—a diverse diet with more fiber and less saturated fat, more

fish and shellfish, smaller portions of well-trimmed meat, vegetables cooked in a manner that preserves vitamins and nutrients—and still a cooking style that exhibits elegance and joy. This is the cuisine of today and of tomorrow; it represents a lower calorie, healthier, more modern, faster, and simpler way of cooking. ❦ In a reflection of life, some of the menus are more concerned with health than others. When we join with friends and family on holidays and special occasions, we sometimes don't count calories—we indulge. At other times we are more careful. I still use butter, salt, and cream, although parsimoniously, adding them in small amounts at the moment when they most influence taste. Essentially this is modern cooking—a blend of substance and sophistication, contemporary food that appeals to everyone. ❦ This kind of cooking avoids gimmicks and trends; rather, it satisfies the tastes of a more discriminating audience while meeting their nutritional needs in a nonprescriptive way. I want a cuisine that appeals to the epicurean and the jogger/sports enthusiast as well as the busy home cook and the single professional. ❦ The ingredients are sometimes listed by weight, sometimes by quantity, and sometimes by unit, depending on which, in my opinion, makes the most sense. For example, I may list "1 banana (about 8 ounces)," yet call for "1 cup sugar." Be sure to read the entire recipe before starting to cook. ❦ As a professional chef, I also want to teach proper cooking techniques and demonstrate how these techniques save time and effort, so that cooking is much more enjoyable. My cuisine is not a complicated or contrived mix of esoteric ingredients, and it is not intended for an elite group of people. It is for everyone. Everyone should know how to defat a stock, how to trim a piece of meat properly, and how to healthfully prepare beef, pork, and other foods not usually associated with lighter cuisine. ❦ Finally, I want to show the importance of togetherness, conviviality, and *joie de vivre* in the kitchen. Cooking should be exciting—nothing compares to the enjoyment of sharing food while spending time with family and friends! But, most of all, I hope that the knowledge readers gain from *Today's Gourmet* will make their lives richer, healthier, and happier.

MENUS

On the following pages I list the twenty-six menus that are featured on my current television series, "Today's Gourmet with Jacques Pépin." Any recipe grouping is arbitrary, influenced by such factors as market availability and personal food preferences. ❧ Use my menus merely as a point of departure. Reorganize as you wish, taking a recipe from one menu and adding it to another. ❧ Although there are only a few salad recipes in the book, you'll note that I have listed salads on most of my menus. We eat salads every day, and I recommend them for taste and balance in a diet. Bread and wine are also part of our daily fare. If you include them with your meals as well, remember to take into account the calories they add. ❧ We don't eat desserts on a regular basis at my house, preferring to end our meals with fresh fruits. I have included dessert recipes here, however, to complete the menus and make them special enough for occasions when you entertain.

From Garden and Grill

Our menu begins with a soufflé that is baked in a gratin dish, making it easy to serve and giving it a beautifully crusty top. This is followed by salmon fillets, cooked just long enough to take on a grilled flavor, and finished in a warm oven. The salmon is served with two accompaniments: asparagus, flavored simply with a little butter and salt; and Portobello mushroom caps, which I grill alongside the salmon. For dessert, we have a sun-dried strawberry jam—for me the best jam in the world—that can be served either as a spread or as a dessert topping. The berries are "cooked" either in the full sun of early summer or in a low-temperature oven, until they become soft and plump and the liquid surrounding them thickens into a syrup.

Spinach, Ham, and Parmesan Soufflé, page 54

Grilled Salmon Fillets, page 80

Ragout of Asparagus, page 108

Grilled Portobello Mushrooms, page 111

Salad

Strawberries in the Sun, page 153

Suggested wine: 1990 Domaine de la Saulzaie Muscadet

A Make-Ahead Menu

I love slowly braised casserole dishes, not only because the long cooking makes the meat in them tender and delicious, but also because they can be prepared almost entirely ahead and served family-style from the pot at the table. This is the case with our breast of veal main course; the meat is braised until fork-tender and then garnished with carrots, onions, and garlic. Preceding the *cocotte* is a dish featuring poached skate, which I serve on top of a fresh beet salad. Some of the beet juice is spooned around the skate, and then it is sprinkled with curry- and cilantro-flavored oils for a stunning presentation and enticing taste. Finally, for dessert, a cobbler makes good use of berries in season. I use blueberries, lightly sweetened with apricot preserves and covered with crumbled pound cake, sponge cake, or cookies before baking.

Skate with Beets and Flavored Oil, page 64

Breast of Veal Cocotte, page 102

Salad

Blueberry Crumble, page 144

For cooking: 1990 La Chiara Gavi

Suggested table wine: 1989 Domaine du Cayron Gigondas

A Budget Feast

Squid, one of the least expensive seafoods and almost waste-free, is our first course. Impaled on skewers and briefly grilled, it is served on watercress. The stems from the watercress can by used for a thrifty soup to be served at another meal. Following the squid we have a small pork roast flavored with honey, ginger, and cayenne pepper, cooked slowly, and served with a dish common to the Lyon area of France where I grew up, julienned potatoes pressed into a compact "cake" and sautéed in a nonstick skillet. A flavorful dessert completes this menu. Frozen vanilla yogurt (or ice cream, as a richer substitute) is topped with Kahlua, dried figs, and chocolate-coated coffee beans.

Grilled Squid on Watercress, page 69

Slow-Cooked Pork Roast, page 94

Darphin Potatoes, page 113

Salad

Frozen Black Velvet, page 142

Suggested wine: 1986 Wolf Blass Cabernet Sauvignon President's Selection

Thrifty Kitchen

Economy in the kitchen is always a concern for me, and a good chef should know how to create beautiful menus with leftover food. I begin this meal with an appealing soup made with pods reserved from peas I shell for the pea and ham stew that I serve later in the meal. Onions, leeks, and potatoes round out the flavor of the soup. I use a relatively inexpensive, lesser known, but tender and juicy cut of beef from the hip—the triangle, which is part of the top sirloin—for the grilled steak main dish, but any other so-called butcher steak, such as hanging tenderloin or oyster steak, can be substituted. The steak is flavored with a *beurre maître d'hôtel*, consisting of a blend of unsalted butter, parsley, lemon juice, and cracked pepper. I end the meal with plums served in individual ramekins, each with a crushed "hat" of crisp, brown phyllo pastry on top.

Pea Pod Soup, page 22

Steak Maître d'Hôtel (Steak with Parsley Butter), page 103

Stew of Peas and Ham, page 112

Salad

Potted Plums with Phyllo Dough, page 152

Suggested wine: 1988 Robert Stemmler Pinot Noir

Midweek Dinner–a Family Meal

In this menu, I combine a hearty, nourishing soup starter with a lighter entrée. The turkey *fricadelles* are made with lean turkey meat, spinach, and other seasonings, and served with a light mushroom and tomato sauce. To add a touch of elegance in the middle of the week, for dessert I serve a mixture of grapefruit and kiwi flavored with a little sauternes-type sweet wine from the Bordeaux region of France.

Sausage, Potato, and Cabbage Soup, page 41

Turkey Fricadelles with Vegetable Sauce, page 90

Salad

Grapefruit and Kiwi Ambrosia, page 146

For cooking: Muscatella—Muscat Doux Naturel

Suggested table wine: 1989 Trimbach Pinot Blanc (White Alsace)

Foods of the Forest

This would be a typical summer menu at my house. I often go foraging in the woods for wild mushrooms and prefer them cooked quickly and served simply, spooned over toast. I follow this with pasta, another summer staple. I sometimes serve it with pesto made with basil from my garden, but here I top it with a fresh red bell pepper sauce flavored with walnuts and parmesan cheese. This makes a nutritious main course, rich in vitamins, minerals, and complex carbohydrates. I finish this great menu with a country-style apple tart, a free-form concoction of thinly rolled dough covered with thinly sliced apples. Baked until the pastry is dark brown and crusty, the tart is best served while lukewarm or at room temperature.

Wild Mushroom Toast, page 50

Red Pepper Pasta with Walnuts, page 72

Salad

Country Apple Tart, page 128

Suggested wine: 1989 Girard Napa Valley Chardonnay

Vegetable Feast

Meat will not be missed in this healthful menu. To start, large, firm summer tomatoes are hollowed out, stuffed with a mixture containing mushrooms, garlic, onion, scallions, and cooked yellow grits, and then baked. Another grain—round *arborio*-type rice—is used in the risotto main dish. Cooked in the conventional way with chicken stock, the rice is extended and flavored with an assortment of vegetables. The meal ends with a mélange of blue cheese and apple sprinkled with black pepper and served with pecans and sprigs of basil or arugula leaves.

Tomatoes Stuffed with Yellow Grits, page 51

Risotto with Vegetables, page 74

Salad

Cheese, Apple, and Nut Mélange, page 130

Suggested wine: 1990 Vernaccia di San Gimignano-Falchini

Personal Favorites

Even though in classic French cooking the salad is served after the meat course, at home in Lyon years ago and now in Connecticut I often start my meal with a salad. That good French-style hard salami called *saucisson* is available now in most parts of the United States, and it is wonderful with salad greens. I cut it into thin slices—about 1 ounce per person—and arrange it around a helping of escarole (as white as possible) that has been tossed with a Dijon-style mustard dressing. I follow this with thinly sliced potatoes that are sautéed raw (*à cru*), rather than after they are cooked. This gives them a distinctive flavor that is ideal with a *fines herbes* omelet—my personal favorite. I especially enjoy this type of omelet in the spring and summer, when I can readily find its classic fresh herb components: parsley, tarragon, chives, and chervil. As a finish for this nostalgic meal, I expand a little on an after-school treat that I enjoyed as a child: a piece of *ficelle* ("string" bread) and dark, bittersweet chocolate, to which I add some seedless grapes and toasted hazelnuts. I roast the nuts ahead and store them still in their shells until serving time, so that they retain the freshly roasted taste.

Salad with Saucisson, page 44

Fines Herbes Omelets, page 75

Potato Sauté à Cru, page 115

Pain au Chocolat and Noisettes (Bread with Chocolate and Hazelnuts), page 131

Suggested wine: 1990 Château de la Chaize Brouilly

Cold Weather Comfort

The intensely flavored daube of beef is a comforting, hearty winter entrée. Lean, gelatinous beef from the shoulder or shank is braised slowly with red wine, herbs, and seasonings, and then garnished with carrots, onions, potatoes, and mushrooms. To begin the menu, a green salad featuring caramelized pecans and apples lends sophistication and interest. The simple but elegant dessert consists of whole strawberries dipped in melted currant jelly to subtly sweeten and intensify their flavor and give them a beautiful sheen.

Composed Salad, page 42

Daube of Beef in Red Wine, page 104

Glazed Strawberries, page 154

Suggested cooking and table wine: 1988 Château du Cèdre Cahors

Summer Elegance

This makes a good Sunday menu for family and friends who want to eat elegant food in a relaxed atmosphere. The meal begins with scallops cooked briefly over intense heat until their exterior is crusty brown. We serve these in a "nest" of cooked scallions and garnish them with a mustard sauce. A classic leg of lamb roast follows. Well defatted, the leg is partially roasted, then patted with a seasoned bread crumb mixture, and returned to the oven until the coating is beautifully crusty. I serve the lamb with its classic companion, potatoes and thinly sliced onions cooked in chicken stock and white wine until most of the liquid is absorbed. To finish, there is an apricot and fig soufflé, made with dried apricots that have been transformed into an intensely flavored puree. Small pieces of fig provide color contrast in the soufflé, which can be served on its own or with yogurt or sour cream.

Scallops in Scallion Nests, page 66

Roasted Leg of Lamb, page 98

Potatoes Boulangère, page 114

Salad

Apricot and Fig Soufflé, page 138

Suggested wine: 1988 Château Fourcas Hosten

Autumn Fare

I spend a few weekends each fall and winter skiing and cooking with friends—many of whom are chefs—at Hunter Mountain in New York. This easy menu, featuring a lamb shank entrée, is typical of the hearty meals we prepare together. The lamb is braised here with Great Northern beans, onions, garlic, and thyme leaves to create a kind of mulligan stew that is served with a salad. Our first course features cauliflower flavored with an interesting sauce containing red onion, parsley, gherkins, anchovy fillets, red wine vinegar, and hard-cooked egg. We finish with seedless Red Flame grapes, cooked in a little fruity red wine, flavored with cinnamon, and served with plain yogurt.

Cauliflower Gribiche, page 45

Lamb Shanks and Beans Mulligan, page 95

Salad

Grapes in Red Wine Sauce, page 148

For cooking: 1989 Laurel Glen Cabernet Sauvignon

Suggested table wine: 1986 Château Greysac Grand Cru Bourgeois

City Fish and Country Fowl

For the first course, we begin with salmon in seaweed. Fresh salmon is available almost everywhere now. I cut completely cleaned pieces of it into strips and then roll each strip in *nori*, which is a Japanese seaweed that has been compressed into sheets. This attractive concoction is then cut into slices, steamed, and served with a light sauce made of lemon juice and rind, balsamic vinegar, and seasonings. The salmon skin, usually discarded, is transformed into a crackling used to garnish the salmon slices. After this esoteric first course, we continue with a classic main dish, boned and stuffed Cornish hens. Bulgur wheat provides the base for a stuffing that includes garlic, onion, jalapeño pepper, and unpeeled pieces of Granny Smith apple. This combination goes particularly well with these little birds, but it is good as a stuffing for chicken and duck, too. A salad and fresh fruit round out this filling menu.

Salmon in Nori, page 62

Stuffed and Roasted Cornish Hens, page 88

Salad

Fruits

Suggested wine: 1990 Buena Vista Chardonnay "Carneros"

Elegant and Modern

Our seafood main dish is both elegant and modern: Each serving is topped with a casually dropped pasta "handkerchief" made of two egg roll wrappers sealed around watercress leaves, which are visible through the cooked wrappers. The dessert, also elegant, consists of pointy-topped meringues served with a pungent, slightly acidic raspberry-orange sauce. The light first course features eggplant prepared in a modern way—grilled—and served with a light sauce on a bed of greens. There is a flavorful assortment of vegetables in this healthful, meatless menu.

Grilled Eggplant on Greens, page 48

Seafood with "Handkerchiefs," page 76

Salad

Prickly Meringues with Fruit Sauce, page 136

Suggested wine: 1990 Mâcon-Lugny les Charmes Chardonnay

Today's Approach to Old Classics

This menu exemplifies one aspect of my philosophy: Reinterpret old recipes in a modern style to produce lighter, lower-calorie dishes. Chicken Kiev is traditionally made with unskinned, boneless chicken breasts that are wrapped around large quantities of herb-seasoned butter, then dipped in beaten eggs—often mixed with cream—coated with bread crumbs, and deep-fried. My version is a world away from the calorie-laden original: The breasts are skinless, they are filled with a mushroom puree containing garlic and herbs, they are coated lightly with milk and a mixture of oiled, seasoned bread crumbs, and they are baked. The "Christmas" oysters first course can, of course, be served at any time of the year when fresh oysters are available, although their presentation—in or out of their shells—on a bed of bright green spinach surrounded by a vivid red bell pepper sauce makes them a perfect holiday dish. A refreshing dessert of prunes cooked in a red wine sauce and served with grapefruit segments finishes the meal.

Christmas Oysters, page 58

Chicken Supreme Kiev-Style, page 84

Bulgur Wheat Pilaf, page 123

Salad

Prunes and Grapefruit in Red Wine Sauce, page 147

For cooking: 1990 Peachy Canyon Zinfandel

Suggested champagnes: 1985 Dom Ruinart Blanc de Blancs;

1985 Bollinger Grande Année Brut; and Veuve Clicquot Ponsardin

Classic and Modern Mix

This is a great summer menu. I adore aspic, especially this classic preparation that includes another favorite food of mine, eggs, which I can eat sensibly here. One egg per person is sufficient in this dish, since each egg is surrounded by an intensely flavored, totally fat-free *gelée* made from a stock flavored with tarragon and containing a little lean ham for color. Contrast is provided by a modern-style entrée of tuna steaks with pepper, a dish that is somewhat like the standard pepper steak made with beef, although for variety I use an assortment of peppercorns here. With a fresh piece of tuna, this preparation is absolutely delicious, especially if the tuna is served slightly rare. I accompany the tuna with a tasty gratin containing cubes of leftover bread, cherry tomatoes, garlic, parsley, olive oil, and parmesan cheese. A fruit dessert is always a welcome finale, and I conclude this meal with fresh, ripe pineapple pieces flavored with lime, honey, and kirsch.

Eggs in Aspic with Tarragon, page 52

Tuna Steaks with Peppercorns, page 82

Gratin of Tomato and Bread, page 116

Salad

Pineapple Delice, page 151

Suggested wine: 1990 Hess Collection Napa Valley Chardonnay

Russian Flavors

Codfish in an interesting and flavorful olive and horseradish sauce begins this Russian-inspired menu. It is followed by chicken thighs prepared with onion, garlic, a little white wine, and coriander leaves and stems. The thighs are served with a julienne of zucchini, briefly sautéed. For dessert, we have a classic *kissel*, a fruit puree made here with astringently flavored cranberries. This is served with plain yogurt or sour cream and decorated with pomegranate seeds and mint.

Codfish in Olive and Horseradish Sauce, page 57

Chicken in Coriander Sauce, page 83

Julienne of Zucchini, page 118

Salad

Russian Cranberry Kissel, page 145

For cooking: 1991 Caymus Vineyards Conundrum White Table Wine

Suggested table wine: 1991 Claiborne & Churchill Dry Gewürztraminer

From the North Sea to North Africa

This menu features couscous, the national stew of Morocco, Algeria, and Tunisia, which takes its name from the wheat grain traditionally served with it. Here, the couscous grain is cooked until light and fluffy and served with its classic stew companion. My version uses a minimum of lamb in combination with kohlrabi, squash, eggplant, carrot, zucchini, and the like, in a broth flavored with a hot sauce called *harissa*. The sauce contains a spicy red pepper paste often used as a seasoning in North Africa. The first course, more European than African, consists of salmon cured in a molasses mixture containing an assortment of spices, among them cumin, nutmeg, and paprika. Fresh and dried fruits are suggested as a light finish to this copious menu.

Cured Salmon in Molasses, page 60

Couscous of Lamb, page 96

Salad

Fresh and Dried Fruits

Suggested wine: 1987 Badia a Coltibuono Chianti Classico Riserva

Provençal Tastes

This menu from the south of France begins with a terrine of eggplant and red bell pepper layered with cheese. Unmolded, it is served with a raw tomato sauce, consisting of ripe tomato chunks, a touch of garlic, olive oil, and vinegar. After this fresh-tasting starter, we have red snapper, a fish common to the Mediterranean, cooked and served with an array of sliced vegetables. As a side dish, cucumbers are stewed and flavored with tarragon. To finish, we offer a "surprise omelet," made mostly of egg whites lightly flavored with egg yolk and vanilla. Shaped like a conventional omelet, it is really a soufflé that is baked on slices of pound cake spread with black currant preserves.

Eggplant and Red Pepper Terrine, page 46

Red Snapper in Brunoise Sauce, page 81

Cucumber with Tarragon, page 110

Salad

Jam Omelet Soufflé, page 141

Suggested wine: 1988 Domaine Tempier Bandol

Vietnamese Flavors

This is one of my wife's favorite menus. She loves to cook Oriental food—Chinese, Japanese, and particularly Vietnamese—since we have so many friends of these nationalities. Her interpretation of Hanoi soup, which begins our menu, is a meal in itself. The most important element in this soup is an intensely flavored stock, made here with oxtail, beef shank, and beef bones. After it is totally defatted, the stock is returned to the stove, and garnishes of napa cabbage, bean sprouts, and rice sticks are cooked in it. Additional garnishes—among them red onion, scallions, hot pepper, and cilantro—are added to the bowls at the table. With the soup we serve a cabbage salad flavored with rice wine vinegar, soy sauce, and oyster sauce to give it an Oriental flavor. We finish with banana tartlets, made from a sweet dough that is covered with a light pastry cream, garnished with banana slices, and glazed with apricot preserves.

Hanoi Soup, page 20

Oriental Savoy Salad, page 119

Banana Tartlets, page 132

Suggested beers: Tsing Tao, Anchor Steam, and La Belle Strasbourgeoise

French Atlantic Cooking

Two of my favorite foods—lobster and artichokes—are served together here. The lobsters are quickly steamed and their meat is removed. Then the shells are returned to the pot and boiled to create an extra dish not in our menu, a full-flavored broth thickened with pasta. The lobster meat is served in artichoke bottoms accompanied by broccoli cooked simply and enhanced with a dash of butter. Endive, braised and garnished with olives, soy sauce, and chives, provides a light and interesting start to the meal. For dessert, ripe pear slices are baked with a crumb topping made of bread, butter, sugar, and pecans. This easy dish makes good use of leftover fruit and bread.

Endive with Olives, page 49

Lobster in Artichoke Bottoms, page 78

Broccoli with Butter, page 109

Salad

Pears au Gratin, page 149

Suggested wine: 1989 Domaine de la Maladiere Chablis

Puerto Rican Connection

One of my wife's specialties, this pork and beans main dish is a testament to her Puerto Rican origins. The quantity of meat per person is relatively small—about 3 ounces—because much of the weight of the pork spareribs she uses here is in the bones. Any leftovers can be quickly transformed into soup in a food processor. Yellow rice is the ideal garnish for the pork and beans. Flavored with orange rind, it derives its beautiful color primarily from achiote (annatto) seeds, a common ingredient in Latin American cooking. We begin this otherwise heavy menu with a light onion soup that is more French than Puerto Rican, a reflection of the diversity in our family. To conclude the meal we have a Caribbean treat that my wife loved as a child: guava paste, which we serve here on toast with cream cheese and mint.

Onion Soup with Vermicelli, page 40

Puerto Rican Pork and Beans, page 92

Yellow Rice with Orange Rind, page 124

Salad

Guava Paste Toast with Mint, page 137

Suggested wines: 1989 Torres Vina Sol; 1988 Torres Coronas

Corner Café Food

A little different from what you might ordinarily prepare at home, this is the type of food you would find at a corner bistro in France. We begin with a salad of fennel, pear, reconstituted dried tomatoes, and toasted pumpkin seeds in a dressing containing sherry vinegar. For an interesting presentation, we serve the salad sandwich-style, between two egg roll wrappers that have been cut into ovals and baked until brown and crisp. Our entrée is a fillet of pork, served with a wonderfully acidic sauce. The pork fillet is very lean, and sautéed briefly it remains quite moist. Ideal with the pork are gnocchi made with a mixture of potato and cream puff dough (*pâte à choux*). For dessert, we have a *granité*, a flavored "ice," featuring good-quality, strong, brewed coffee that is frozen and then broken into granulated pieces for serving.

Fennel and Pear Salad, page 43

Fillet of Pork Charcutière, page 93

Gnocchi Maison, page 120

Café au Lait Granité, page 139

Suggested wine: 1989 Bouchaine Pinot Noir "Carneros"

A Melting Pot Menu

We draw from different parts of the world for this menu. It begins with a squid salad inspired by a Vietnamese chef friend and duplicated many times by my wife. Fat-free, it is low-calorie and spicy, containing hot Thai peppers, onion, and garlic, along with mint and lime juice. The main dish reflects Russian influences; ground veal is combined with bread crumbs, garlic, parsley, onion, and milk, and formed into patties, called *bitochki*. These are steamed and served with a horseradish-yogurt sauce that makes the dish flavorfully redolent of Russian cuisine. Finally, we return to America for a cookie horn, filled with fresh and dried fruit flavored with lemon juice and sugar.

Squid Salad à la Binh, page 68

Veal Bitochki, page 99

Salad

Crunchy Horns with Fruit, page 134

Suggested wine: 1991 St. Clement Sauvignon Blanc

A Pépin Potpourri

I often entertain food industry people in my home, and I like to create unusual menus for them that showcase an interesting mix of foods. Here, my first course is a flavorful South American dish—seviche—which I make with scallops and a large assortment of vegetables and herbs. There is no oil in my version of this classic, so it is a lean, clean dish for summer. The main course fricassee is made with large pieces of veal from the shoulder, chuck, or shank. It is garnished with onions and an abundance of mushrooms, and it contains a small amount of cream, added as a final enrichment. I accompany this with wehani rice, a reddish brown, California-grown variety that is elastic, chewy, and delicious served with pumpkin seeds, as it is here. I finish this meal with a light custard topped with a sauce of blueberries, cognac, and apricot preserves.

Scallop Seviche, page 67

Fricassee of Veal, page 100

Wehani Brown Rice, page 125

Salad

Custard with Blueberry Sauce, page 143

Suggested wine: 1989 Fetzer Barrel Select Zinfandel

Menu for a Sunday Gathering

This meal brings back memories of my childhood. Along with fresh mushrooms, which were the main ingredient in my mother's mushroom soup, I use dried mushrooms, because they bring a great intensity of flavor to this simple first course soup. I also flavor it with a leek, thicken it with a potato, and finish it with milk instead of cream, the more traditional but richer choice of most fancy restaurants. The soup is followed by what is for me the ultimate chicken dish: a whole chicken roasted in a very hot oven until the skin is crisp and brown and the flesh moist and succulent. In this menu, the natural juices and a little of the fat that emerge from the chicken as it cooks are combined with pasta shells flavored with swiss cheese. After a salad, I offer a dessert recipe from my youth: crêpes, hot from the pan, spread with a good-quality jam (or sprinkled with a little granulated sugar or grated chocolate), folded, and eaten immediately.

Dried and Fresh Mushroom Soup, page 19

Poulet Rôti (Roasted Chicken), page 86

Coquillettes au Gruyère (Pasta Shells with Swiss Cheese), page 122

Salad

Crêpes à la Confiture, page 140

Suggested wine: 1988 Saint-Joseph Côtes du Rhône

Special Guest Menu

This is a special menu not only because the recipes are a bit more elegant than those for everyday but also because they contain more costly ingredients. Veal chops, for example, are expensive, but for a special occasion they are delicate and delicious, grilled and served with a caper sauce. Vegetable burgers, composed of an assortment of vegetables bound together with cooked grits, make an interesting and succulent accompaniment. As a first course, striped bass—either whole or in fillets—are cooked in a flavorful vegetable and wine mixture. We conclude with a light dessert of pears cooked in espresso and flavored with lemon rind and Kahlua.

Nage Courte of Striped Bass, page 56

Grilled Veal Chops with Caper Sauce, page 101

Vegetable Burgers, page 117

Salad

Pears in Espresso, page 150

For cooking: 1990 Murphy-Goode Chardonnay

Suggested table wine: 1990 Merryvale Napa Valley Chardonnay Starmont

Special Segments

In most of the "Today's Gourmet" shows, when time allows, I like to do a "special segment" that emphasizes a key point or demonstrates a technique. These are the twenty-one special segments in season two of the television program.

A Make-Ahead Menu
Making flavored oils

A Budget Feast
Cleaning squid

Thrifty Kitchen
Shelling peas and preparing beans for cooking

Midweek Dinner—a Family Meal
Preparing Grapefruit and Kiwi Ambrosia dessert

Foods of the Forest
Discussion of wild and dried mushrooms

Cold Weather Comfort
Preparing glazed strawberries

Autumn Fare
Discussion of hard-cooked eggs

City Fish and Country Fowl
Boning a Cornish hen

Elegant and Modern
Rolling out wonton skins filled with watercress leaves

Today's Approach to Old Classics
Discussion of oysters

Classic and Modern Mix
Molding aspic

Russian Flavors
Discussion of cookware

From the North Sea to North Africa
Boning a salmon and explaining gravlax

Provençal Tastes
Roasting and peeling peppers

Vietnamese Flavors
Discussion of oriental sauces and macerating cabbage

French Atlantic Cooking
Preparing artichoke bottoms

Puerto Rican Connection
Making soup from pork and beans leftovers

A Melting Pot Menu
Freezing herb packets

A Pépin Potpourri
Discussion of bouquets garni and herbes de Provence

Menu for a Sunday Gathering
Carving and reconstructing chicken

Special Guest Menu
Discussion of veal chops

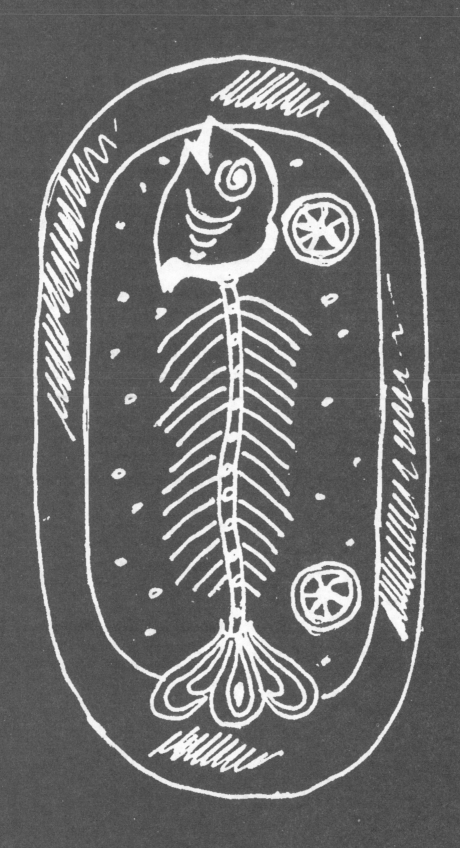

FIRST COURSES

Lobster Broth with Pasta, page 18

Dried and Fresh Mushroom Soup, page 19

Hanoi Soup, page 20

Pea Pod Soup, page 22

Watercress Soup, page 39

Onion Soup with Vermicelli, page 40

Sausage, Potato, and Cabbage Soup, page 41

Composed Salad, page 42

Fennel and Pear Salad, page 43

Salad with Saucisson, page 44

Cauliflower Gribiche, page 45

Eggplant and Red Pepper Terrine, page 46

Grilled Eggplant on Greens, page 48

Endive with Olives, page 49

Wild Mushroom Toast, page 50

Tomatoes Stuffed with Yellow Grits, page 51

Eggs in Aspic with Tarragon, page 52

Spinach, Ham, and Parmesan Soufflé, page 54

Nage Courte of Striped Bass, page 56

Codfish in Olive and Horseradish Sauce, page 57

Christmas Oysters, page 58

Cured Salmon in Molasses, page 60

Salmon in Nori, page 62

Skate with Beets and Flavored Oil, page 64

Scallops in Scallion Nests, page 66

Scallop Seviche, page 67

Squid Salad à la Binh, page 68

Grilled Squid on Watercress, page 69

Lobster Broth with Pasta

his is one way of extending a recipe. When preparing Lobster in Artichoke Bottoms, page 78, I reserve the lobster cooking liquid. This broth can be frozen and used as needed. Reduced, it makes a simple and delicious soup with the addition of pastina, or, if you prefer, angel hair pasta or rice.

6 cups lobster broth (from Lobster in Artichoke Bottoms, page 78)

½ cup pastina

½ teaspoon freshly ground black pepper

Salt to taste (amount depending on saltiness of broth)

2 tablespoons chopped chives

Bring the broth to a boil in a stainless steel saucepan. Add the pastina and stir well. Bring the broth back to a boil, cover, and boil gently for about 10 minutes, until the pastina is very tender. Add the pepper and the salt to taste. Ladle the soup into four soup bowls and sprinkle with chives. Serve immediately.

Yield: 4 servings

Nutritional analysis per serving: calories 77; protein 3 gm.; carbohydrates 15 gm.; fat 0.3 gm.; saturated fat 0.04 gm.; cholesterol 0 mg.; sodium 195 mg.

Dried and Fresh Mushroom Soup

ried mushrooms are responsible for the great intensity of flavor in this soup, although fresh mushrooms—primarily stem pieces—help create the base for the soup and their caps are used as a garnish. The soup can be made richer with the addition of cream at the end, and it can be served cold as well as hot.

½ ounce dried cèpe mushrooms (½ cup)

1 cup milk

4 ounces fresh mushrooms, cleaned

1½ teaspoons virgin olive oil

1 medium onion (about 3 ounces), peeled and cut into ½-inch cubes

1 small leek (about 3 ounces), cleaned and thinly sliced

1 medium to large potato (about 6 ounces), peeled and cut into ½-inch cubes

1 teaspoon salt

Soak the dried mushrooms in the milk for at least 1 hour. Drain, reserving the milk. Cut enough of the fresh mushroom caps into julienne strips to measure ¾ cup. Set aside.

Heat the olive oil in a large saucepan. When it is hot, add the onion and leek and sauté for 2 minutes over low heat. Add the cèpe mushrooms, potato, salt, remaining fresh mushroom pieces, and 2½ cups water. Bring to a boil, cover, reduce the heat to low, and simmer gently for 25 minutes.

Puree the soup in the saucepan using a hand blender or puree it in a food processor and return it to the saucepan. Add the julienned mushroom caps and bring to a boil. At serving time, stir in the reserved milk, bring to a boil, and serve immediately.

Yield: 4 servings (5 cups)

Nutritional analysis per serving: calories 115; protein 4 gm.; carbohydrates 17 gm.; fat 4.0 gm.; saturated fat 1.5 gm.; cholesterol 9 mg.; sodium 589 mg.

Hanoi Soup

This is my wife's rendition of a classic Vietnamese soup. One of my favorites, it is a meal in itself, quite satisfying on a cold winter night. The esoteric ingredients—star anise, rice sticks, and *nuoc mam*—are available in Asian markets and can also be found in the Asian section of many supermarkets. ❦ The base of this soup is a very good stock made with oxtail, beef shank, and beef bones. It is flavored with star anise, ginger, and shallots that have been held over a gas flame or hot electric burner until well charred on all sides. In addition to giving the stock a rich color, the burned shallots impart a very specific taste. ❦ This colorful soup should be served in large (2- to 3-cup capacity) bowls to accommodate all the garnishes. There is enough here for four generous or six smaller servings.

1½ pounds oxtail, cut into 2- or 3-inch pieces

1½ pounds beef shank (about 2 slices, each 1 inch thick, with bones)

1 pound beef bones, cut into 3-inch pieces

3 whole shallots, peeled (about 3 ounces)

1 piece ginger (about 2 inches), unpeeled

3 pieces star anise

1 thin cinnamon stick (about 3 inches long)

1 teaspoon salt

For the garnishes

1½ cups bean sprouts (6 ounces)

5 ounces rice sticks (rice vermicelli)

1½ cups freshly shredded napa cabbage

Fish sauce (nuoc mam)

1 cup (loosely packed) cilantro (coriander or Chinese parsley)

1 cup red onion, very finely sliced

2 tablespoons hot pepper, seeded and sliced

4 scallions, cleaned and minced (½ cup)

1 lime, cut into 4 wedges

Place the oxtail, shank, beef bones, and 6 quarts cold water in a stainless steel stockpot. Bring to a boil over high heat. (This will take 25 to 30 minutes.) Skim off and discard any impurities that rise to the surface and continue to cook at a fairly high boil for 5 minutes, removing surface scum as it collects. Reduce the heat to low.

Impale the shallots and ginger on a skewer and hold them over the flames of a gas stove or directly above the heated burner of an electric stove for about 5 minutes, turning them often, until they are charred on all sides. Add to the stock with the anise stars and cinnamon, and boil the mixture very gently for 4 hours.

Remove the bones and meat to a bowl and strain the liquid twice through a paper-towel-lined strainer to eliminate the fat. (You will have 8 to 9 cups.)

Wash the stockpot, return the stock to it, and add the salt. Pick the meat from the bones, eliminating any fat and sinew, and break it into pieces. (You will have about 3 cups.) Set aside.

For the garnishes: Bring 3 cups water to a boil and add the bean sprouts. Cook for $3\frac{1}{2}$ to 4 minutes, until the mixture comes back to a strong boil. Drain.

Bring 6 cups water to a boil. Add the rice sticks and bring back to a boil. Boil for about $2\frac{1}{2}$ minutes, until tender. Drain in a colander and run briefly under cold water to cool.

At serving time, bring the stock to a boil. Heat the meat in a microwave oven or with a little stock in a saucepan on top of the stove. Place some of the rice sticks, shredded cabbage, bean sprouts, and meat in each of four large bowls (2- to 3-cup capacity), and fill the bowls with the boiling stock. Bring to the table and pass around the fish sauce, cilantro, red onion, hot pepper, and scallions. Each diner can add as much of these ingredients as desired. Squeeze the juice of a lime wedge over each bowl and eat the soup immediately.

Yield: 4 servings

Nutritional analysis per serving: calories 252; protein 37 gm.; carbohydrates 6 gm.; fat 8.2 gm.; saturated fat 2.4 gm.; cholesterol 83 mg.; sodium 628 mg.

Pea Pod Soup

This is a bonus recipe, made with the pods from the fresh peas shelled for the Stew of Peas and Ham, page 112. Be sure to sort through the pods and discard any that are damaged before proceeding. ❧ It is absolutely essential that you strain this soup through a food mill before serving it. Pea pods are, of course, full of inedible fiber, but they also contain soft flesh, which is extruded when the pods are pushed through the food mill. Using a food processor and then straining the mixture through a conventional strainer is not a good alternative. ❧ For a richer soup, add some light or heavy cream to the completed recipe and serve with croutons, if desired.

1½ teaspoons corn oil

1 onion (about 4 ounces), peeled and cut into 1-inch pieces

1 leek (about 5 ounces), cleaned and cut (greens and all) into 1-inch pieces

¾ teaspoon salt

4 or 5 potatoes (12 ounces total), peeled and cut into 2-inch pieces

10 ounces fresh pea pods, reserved from peas shelled for Stew of Peas and Ham, page 112

1 tablespoon unsalted butter

Croutons, for garnish (optional)

Heat the oil in a saucepan and add the onion and leek. Cook for 2 to 3 minutes over medium to high heat. Add 3 cups water, the salt, and the potatoes, and bring to a boil.

Meanwhile, wash the pods and discard any damaged ones. Add the pods to the saucepan, bring the mixture to a boil again, and boil, covered, for 30 minutes. Push the mixture through a food mill. (You should have about 5½ cups.) Add the butter and mix until it has melted. Serve the soup as is or with croutons, if desired.

Yield: 4 servings (about 5½ cups)

Nutritional analysis per serving: calories 148; protein 4 gm.; carbohydrates 23 gm.; fat 4.9 gm.; saturated fat 2.0 gm.; cholesterol 8 mg.; sodium 425 mg.

Top: Cheese, Apple, and Nut Mélange (see page 130). Below: Pain au Chocolat and Noisettes (see page 131).

Hanoi Soup (see page 20), with its garnishes.

Eggplant and Red Pepper Terrine (see page 46).

Top: Seafood with "Handkerchiefs" (see page 76). Below: Codfish in Olive and Horseradish Sauce (see page 57).

Top: Grilled Squid on Watercress (see page 69). Below: Scallop Seviche (see page 67).

Top: Scallops in Scallion Nests (see page 66). Below: Red Snapper in Brunoise Sauce (see page 81), accompanied by Cucumber with Tarragon (see page 110).

Lobster in Artichoke Bottoms (see page 78), accompanied by Broccoli with Butter (see page 109).

Top: Cured Salmon in Molasses (see page 60). Below: Salmon in Nori (see page 62).

Stuffed and Roasted Cornish Hens (see page 88).

Top: Roasted Leg of Lamb (see page 98). Below: Lamb Shanks and Beans Mulligan (see page 95).

Top: Chicken Supreme Kiev-Style (see page 84). Below: Fillet of Pork Charcutière (see page 93), accompanied by Gnocchi Maison (see page 120).

Top: Grilled Veal Chops with Caper Sauce (see page 101). Below: Gratin of Tomato and Bread (see page 116).

Daube of Beef in Red Wine (see page 104).

**Top: Potted Plums with Phyllo Dough (see page 152). Below: Custard with
Blueberry Sauce (see page 143).**

Crêpes à la Confiture (see page 140), garnished with fresh fruit and mint leaves.

Top: Grapefruit and Kiwi Ambrosia (see page 146). Right: Russian Cranberry Kissel (see page 145). Lower left: Frozen Black Velvet (see page 142).

Watercress Soup

This thrifty recipe makes use of the stems of the watercress leaves I used in Grilled Squid on Watercress, page 69. Sometimes tough and often strong-flavored, the stems are ideal for soup. ❧ Since the soup will be pureed, the vegetables need only be coarsely cut before they are added to the pot. The mixture can be transferred to a food processor or food mill for pureeing, but, to save time and labor, a hand blender immersed directly into the cooking pot works well here. ❧ This soup freezes well and can be served cold as well as hot. With the addition of cream or milk, the cold soup can be transformed into a type of vichyssoise.

1 tablespoon canola oil

4 ounces watercress stems (reserved from Grilled Squid on Watercress, page 69), washed

1 stalk celery (2 ounces), coarsely diced (about 1 cup)

1 onion (6 ounces), coarsely diced (about 2 cups)

2 cloves garlic, peeled

2½ cups homemade stock (chicken, beef, veal, or a mixture of these)

¾ teaspoon salt (more or less, depending on the saltiness of the stock)

¾ pound potatoes, peeled and cut into 2-inch pieces

Croutons, for garnish (optional)

Heat the oil in a saucepan. When it is hot, add the watercress stems, celery, onion, and garlic, and cook for 2 minutes. Add the stock, salt, and potatoes, and bring the mixture to a boil. Cover, reduce the heat, and boil gently for 30 minutes.

Puree the mixture either with a hand-held blender in the pot, or by pushing it through a food mill or processing it in a food processor.

Serve the soup hot, garnished, if desired, with croutons.

Yield: 4 servings

Nutritional analysis per serving: calories 127; protein 4 gm.; carbohydrates 18 gm.; fat 4.5 gm.; saturated fat 0.5 gm.; cholesterol 0 mg.; sodium 544 mg.

Onion Soup with Vermicelli

T his is one of those easy, quickly prepared soups that we often make at home when we feel like eating soup and have no time to cook. I like it when the onions are cooked for long enough over high heat to become a rich, dark-brown color. ❦ To make a standard onion soup, a *gratinée*, omit the pasta and chives, top each bowl of soup with two or three toasted *baguette* slices and some grated Gruyère cheese, and place the bowls in a 400-degree oven until the cheese on top is crusty and brown. This is very good, certainly, although much more caloric than the rendition that follows.

1 tablespoon corn oil

4 medium onions (1 pound total), peeled and sliced thin

6 cups light chicken or beef broth, or a mixture of both, preferably homemade and salt-free

¾ teaspoon salt

¼ teaspoon freshly ground black pepper

⅔ cup (2 ounces) vermicelli (angel hair pasta)

2 tablespoons minced chives

Heat the oil until it is hot but not smoking. Add the onions and sauté them over medium to high heat for 10 to 12 minutes, until they are soft and a rich, dark-brown color.

Add the stock, salt, and pepper. Bring the mixture to a boil, cover, and boil for 5 minutes. Add the pasta, bring back to a boil, cover, and boil gently for 5 minutes. Divide among four bowls, sprinkle with chives, and serve.

Yield: 4 servings (6 cups)

Nutritional analysis per serving: calories 168; protein 6 gm.; carbohydrates 22 gm.; fat 6.1 gm.; saturated fat 1.1 gm.; cholesterol 0 mg.; sodium 496 mg.

Sausage, Potato, and Cabbage Soup

I t's worthwhile to make a large batch of this soup and freeze the remainder for another meal. Followed by a salad, it makes an ideal lunch on a cold winter day. This soup is high in vitamin C and potassium. If you are concerned about your calorie intake, use only half the amount of sausage called for here or eliminate the sausage entirely for a different but still delicious result. Leftovers can be reheated again and again, and they taste better every time.

8 ounces coarsely ground sausage meat

½ pound onions, peeled and cut into 1-inch slices (1½ cups)

6 scallions, cut into ½-inch pieces (1¼ cups)

1 pound potatoes, peeled and cut into ½-inch slices

8 ounces savoy cabbage, cut into 1½-inch pieces (4 cups)

1¼ teaspoons salt

French bread

Break the sausage meat into pieces and place it in a saucepan over high heat. Sauté for 10 minutes, stirring and scraping the bottom of the pan with a spoon to keep the meat from sticking, until the sausage is well browned.

Add the onions and scallions and cook for 1 minute. Stir in 6 cups water, the potatoes, the cabbage, and the salt. Bring to a boil, cover, reduce the heat to low, and cook for 45 minutes.

Serve the soup in bowls (there will be about 10 cups, or 1¼ cups per serving) with chunks of crusty French bread.

Yield: 8 servings (about 10 cups)

Nutritional analysis per serving: calories 174; protein 5 gm.; carbohydrates 13 gm.; fat 11.5 gm.; saturated fat 4.1 gm.; cholesterol 19 mg.; sodium 545 mg.

Composed Salad

A composed salad consists of greens and any of an almost endless variety of other ingredients, from cooked vegetables to fruits, nuts, poultry, lamb, beef, fish, and shellfish. Depending on the contents, the salad can be served cold, lukewarm, or at room temperature, as either a first or a main course. ❦ In this version, I add cheese, apple, and caramelized pecans to curly endive or escarole. The combination makes this composed salad an ideal summer supper or lunch main course or elegant dinner first course.

For the spicy caramelized pecans

¼ cup pecan halves

½ teaspoon canola oil

1 tablespoon sugar

Dash of salt

Dash of cayenne pepper

1 medium apple (about 4 ounces), preferably russet or golden delicious

1½ teaspoons lemon juice

For the sherry vinaigrette

1½ tablespoons oil (a mixture of walnut, hazelnut, and/or canola)

1½ teaspoons sherry vinegar

⅛ teaspoon salt

¼ teaspoon freshly ground black pepper

4 cups salad greens (preferably the white center of curly endive or escarole), cut into 1½- to 2-inch pieces, washed and thoroughly dried in a salad spinner

1 ounce semi-dry or hard goat cheese, crumbled into pieces about ½-inch in size

For the pecans: Place the pecans in a skillet and cover (barely) with water. Bring to a simmer over high heat and drain immediately. Place the pecans back in the pan with the oil, sugar, salt, and cayenne. Cook over medium to high heat, stirring until the nuts brown and the mixture caramelizes. Transfer the pecans to a plate to cool.

For the apple: Wash the apple, halve it, and remove the core. Cut it into ½-inch slices. Then, stack the slices and cut them into ½-inch strips. Mix the apple strips with the lemon juice and set them aside.

Mix the sherry vinaigrette ingredients together in a salad bowl.

At serving time, toss the greens with the vinaigrette and arrange on individual plates. Sprinkle with the apple strips, crumbled cheese, and pecans. Serve immediately.

Yield: 4 servings

Nutritional analysis per serving: calories 153; protein 2 gm.; carbohydrates 10 gm.; fat 12.1 gm.; saturated fat 0.8 gm.; cholesterol 0 mg.; sodium 184 mg.

Fennel and Pear Salad

T his elegant salad is sandwiched between crisp egg roll wrappers, which give the dish texture and make a very attractive presentation. ❦ The wrappers are available packaged in the produce section of most supermarkets. These thin, low-calorie pastry sheets can also be brushed with oil, baked until crisp, and served with cheese in place of toast or bread. ❦ This salad has diverse ingredients—reconstituted dried tomatoes, fennel, pumpkin seeds, and pears—but the distinctive flavor of each is delightful in combination with the others.

1 teaspoon corn, peanut, or canola oil

8 egg roll wrappers, each cut to form an oval 4½ inches long by 3 inches wide

¼ cup pumpkin seeds

½ cup dried tomatoes (about 1 ounce)

1 small fennel bulb (about 10 ounces), thinly sliced (about 2½ cups), with stem removed and fuzzy leaves (about ¼ cup) set aside for decoration

1 Bosc pear (about 5 ounces), peeled, cored, and cut into ½-inch pieces

For the sherry vinaigrette

2 tablespoons virgin olive oil

1 tablespoon sherry vinegar

¼ teaspoon salt

¼ teaspoon freshly ground black pepper

Preheat the oven to 400 degrees. Brush a cookie sheet lightly with ½ teaspoon of the oil. Arrange the egg roll ovals on the sheet and brush the tops of them with the remaining ½ teaspoon of oil. Bake at 400 degrees until brown and crisp, about 6 to 7 minutes. Transfer to a plate and set aside until serving time.

Spread the pumpkin seeds on a cookie sheet and toast them lightly in a 400-degree oven for about 4 or 5 minutes. Set aside. Bring 2 cups water to a boil in a saucepan, drop in the dried tomatoes, and bring back to a boil. Cover the pan and set it off the heat for 10 minutes. Drain, reserving the cooking liquid in the refrigerator or freezer for use in soups or stews. Cut the tomatoes into 1-inch pieces.

Bring 1 quart water to a boil. Add the fennel and cook it over high heat for about 3 minutes, or just until the water returns to a boil. Drain and cool for a few minutes.

In a bowl, gently mix together the fennel, pear, and tomato pieces with the pumpkin seeds and all the vinaigrette ingredients.

To serve, place an egg roll crisp on each of four plates. Spoon the fennel mixture on top of the crisps and top each serving with another egg roll crisp to create a salad "sandwich." Garnish with the reserved fennel leaves and serve immediately.

Yield: 4 servings

Nutritional analysis per serving: calories 294; protein 9 gm.; carbohydrates 43 gm.; fat 10.3 gm.; saturated fat 1.4 gm.; cholesterol 39 mg.; sodium 217 mg.

Salad with Saucisson

 This salad with a garlicky mustard vinaigrette is classic in French bistros, where it is enjoyed as a light lunch or a snack, either during the day or after the theater. It is traditionally served with slices of pâté or a good hard salami, called *saucisson* in French. A crusty *baguette* is the perfect accompaniment.

4 ounces good quality, hard French saucisson salami

1 large head escarole, as white as possible, cut into 1½-inch pieces (about 8 cups)

For the garlic-Dijon vinaigrette

2 cloves garlic, cut into very small dice (about 2 teaspoons)

¼ teaspoon freshly ground black pepper

¼ teaspoon salt

2 teaspoons Dijon-style mustard

1 tablespoon red wine vinegar

2 tablespoons peanut oil

Crusty bread

Remove the "skin" or casing from the *saucisson* and cut it into about 20 very thin slices (about 5 slices per person).

Wash the escarole thoroughly, dipping it up and down in a sink filled with cold water, and dry it in a salad spinner to remove moisture that would otherwise dilute the vinaigrette.

For the garlic-Dijon vinaigrette: In the bowl you will use for serving the salad, mix together all the vinaigrette ingredients. The mixture should not be homogenized; the ingredients should separate somewhat.

At serving time, add the escarole to the bowl and toss it thoroughly with the vinaigrette. Divide it among four plates and arrange the *saucisson* slices around the periphery of each plate. Serve with crusty bread.

Yield: 4 servings

Nutritional analysis per serving: calories 201; protein 8 gm.; carbohydrates 5 gm.; fat 16.9 gm.; saturated fat 4.6 gm.; cholesterol 22 mg.; sodium 760 mg.

Cauliflower Gribiche

I enjoy eating this dish with a chunk of bread for lunch, but it also makes a great dinner first course or salad course and can even be served as a snack. I love cauliflower and find it particularly appealing garnished with red onion and anchovy fillets, a combination that is high in vitamin C and potassium. ❦ The *gribiche* should be served at room temperature. If you make it ahead and refrigerate it, take the chill off by heating it momentarily in a microwave oven.

---

1 head cauliflower (1¼ to 1½ pounds), without greens

1 large egg

¼ cup sour gherkins, coarsely chopped

⅓ cup coarsely chopped parsley

⅓ cup diced (¼-inch dice) red onion

1 can (2 ounces) anchovy fillets, cut into ¼-inch pieces

1 tablespoon red wine vinegar

2 tablespoons virgin olive oil

½ teaspoon salt

½ teaspoon freshly ground black pepper

Separate the cauliflower into flowerets and cut each floweret into pieces about 1 inch across at the flower. (You should have about 6 cups.)

Place the cauliflower in a large saucepan and add 1 cup water. Bring the water to a strong boil, cover, and cook over high heat for 3 to 4 minutes, until the water has evaporated. Transfer the cauliflower to a bowl.

Bring 2 cups water to a boil in a small saucepan. Carefully lower the egg into the water, cover, reduce the heat, and boil gently for 9 minutes. Immediately pour out the hot water and replace it with ice water. Cool the egg completely. Then peel it and cut it into ¼-inch pieces.

Add all the remaining ingredients except the egg to the cauliflower in the bowl and mix. Transfer the mixture to a serving platter, sprinkle the egg on top, and serve immediately.

Yield: 4 servings

Nutritional analysis per serving: calories 149; protein 8 gm.; carbohydrates 10 gm.; fat 9.5 gm.; saturated fat 1.6 gm.; cholesterol 59 mg.; sodium 931 mg.

Eggplant and Red Pepper Terrine

S erving eight people, this is an ideal dish for a summer party. I like to use narrow eggplants that are about as long as my mold, which is 11 inches long, 4 inches wide, and 3 inches high, so I can make nice layers with lengthwise strips of the eggplant. The paler Japanese eggplants work well here, but if you don't have access to them, just select regular eggplants that are somewhat long and thin. The peppers and eggplants can be cooked and the dish assembled a day ahead. The terrine should not be unmolded, however, until just before serving. ❦ I use Brie with the eggplant; it is flavorful and easy to cut into the thin strips I need in the terrine. Another cheese—mozzarella, for example—can be substituted, although it may be harder to slice thinly. Or, if you want to reduce the calorie count of this dish further, eliminate the cheese altogether. ❦ The raw tomato sauce is easy to make and could also be served on its own as a cold tomato gazpacho soup.

3 large red bell peppers (about 1½ pounds)

2 large, long (11-inch), firm eggplants (about 2½ pounds)

2 tablespoons peanut oil

1½ cups (loose) flat-leaf parsley leaves

¾ teaspoon salt

½ teaspoon freshly ground black pepper

8 ounces firm Brie cheese, cut into ⅛-inch slices (about 14 slices)

For the raw tomato sauce

3 cloves garlic, peeled

2 to 3 ripe tomatoes (1¼ pounds), each cut into 6 to 8 pieces

¼ cup virgin olive oil

2 tablespoons red wine vinegar

½ teaspoon salt

¼ teaspoon freshly ground black pepper

¼ teaspoon Tabasco sauce

Arrange the red peppers on a tray and place them under a hot broiler so that their upper surfaces are about 1/2 inch from the heat. Broil for 15 minutes, turning occasionally, until the peppers are blistered and black on all sides. Immediately transfer them to a large plastic bag and seal or tie the bag shut. Let the peppers "steam" in their own residual heat inside the bag for 10 minutes. Then peel them (the skin will slide off), split them, and seed them under cool running water. Dry the flesh with paper towels.

Heat a grill until very hot. Cut the eggplants lengthwise into 1/2-inch slices (10 to 12 total), brush the slices on both sides with the peanut oil, and sprinkle with half the salt. Cook the eggplant slices on the grill, covered, for 4 minutes on each side, until they are nicely browned and soft. (If your grill does not have a lid, make a tentlike lid of aluminum foil and place it over the eggplant as it cooks.)

While the eggplant is grilling, soften the parsley by blanching it in boiling water for 5 to 10 seconds. Remove, cool under cold water, and drain.

Line a terrine mold (loaf or pâté pan) with plastic wrap. Arrange a layer of eggplant in the bottom of the mold and top it with about a third each of the red pepper pieces, parsley, remaining salt, pepper, and cheese. Repeat, beginning and ending with a layer of eggplant, until all the ingredients are used. Cover with plastic wrap and press on the wrap to compact the mixture. Refrigerate.

For the sauce: Place the garlic in the bowl of a food processor and process for 10 seconds. Add the tomatoes and process until pureed. Push the mixture through a food mill (fitted with a fine screen) set over a bowl. Add 1/3 cup water and the remainder of the sauce ingredients. Mix well.

To serve, pour some of the sauce on a large platter and unmold the terrine in the center. Cut it into slices and serve with the remainder of the sauce.

Yield: 8 servings

Nutritional analysis per serving: calories 261; protein 9 gm.; carbohydrates 18 gm.; fat 18.5 gm.; saturated fat 1.5 gm.; cholesterol 28 mg.; sodium 540 mg.

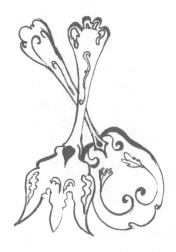

Grilled Eggplant on Greens

T he smaller, sweeter Japanese eggplants are ideal for this dish, but if they are not available use the standard American variety. My family loves the unique taste that grilling gives eggplant, and this simple recipe makes an ideal first course for a summer meal. I especially like the eggplant served on young home-grown greens such as radicchio and arugula. Their slightly bitter flavor offsets the natural sweetness of the eggplant.

2 small, firm eggplants, preferably the long, narrow Japanese variety (about 1 pound total)

1 tablespoon canola oil

½ teaspoon salt

2 tablespoons virgin olive oil

1 tablespoon soy sauce

1 tablespoon rice vinegar

3 cups (loose) mixed salad greens, thoroughly washed and dried

Cut off the top and bottom ends of the eggplants and cut them lengthwise into ½-inch slices. (You should have about 8 slices.) Rub the slices on both sides with the canola oil and sprinkle them with the salt.

Heat a grill until very hot. Place the eggplant slices on the grill and cook for 3 minutes on each side.

Meanwhile, combine the olive oil, soy sauce, and vinegar in a small bowl.

Arrange the salad greens on a platter and place the grilled eggplant slices on top. Pour the sauce over both and serve immediately.

Yield: 4 servings

Nutritional analysis per serving: calories 129; protein 2 gm.; carbohydrates 9 gm.; fat 10.4 gm.; saturated fat 1.2 gm.; cholesterol 0 mg.; sodium 539 mg.

Endive with Olives

his easy recipe is attractive and delicious as a light first course or as an accompaniment to grilled meat or grilled or broiled fish. It is ready in a few minutes, and the combination of flavors—bitter endive with garlic, olives, and soy sauce—makes it an interesting and unusual dish.

2 large endives (about ¾ pound total), thoroughly washed, drained, and quartered lengthwise

2 cloves garlic, peeled, crushed, and chopped (1 teaspoon)

1½ tablespoons virgin olive oil

1 tablespoon red wine vinegar

¼ teaspoon salt

¼ teaspoon freshly ground black pepper

2 tablespoons coarsely chopped black olives

1 teaspoon light soy sauce

1 tablespoon chopped chives

Place all the ingredients except the olives, soy sauce, and chives in a stainless steel saucepan with ½ cup water. Bring the mixture to a boil, cover, reduce the heat to low, and boil gently for 10 minutes. Stir in the olives and the soy sauce, and divide among six plates, allowing two pieces of endive per plate. Sprinkle with the chives and serve.

Yield: 4 servings

Nutritional analysis per serving: calories 65; protein 1 gm.; carbohydrates 4 gm.; fat 5.6 gm.; saturated fat 0.7 gm.; cholesterol 0 mg.; sodium 228 mg.

Wild Mushroom Toast

This is one of my favorite first courses in summer, when I often go mushrooming in the woods with my wife and daughter, my friends, or sometimes just my dog. If you don't know wild mushrooms, I would strongly advise against picking them on your own. Mycological societies throughout the country organize tours, however, and, if this activity appeals to you, contact the society nearest to you, and go on a hunt with people who are knowledgeable about wild mushrooms. It's great fun, and the rewards are terrific; wild mushrooms you find yourself are free, while those you buy in specialty stores are quite expensive. 🦃 I use a mixture of domestic and wild mushrooms here. I spoon them over toast, but this recipe would also be good as a garnish for steak or grilled veal or lamb chops. Low in calories, mushrooms are a good source of potassium.

2 tablespoons unsalted butter

1 tablespoon virgin olive oil

1 pound mixed domestic and wild mushrooms (King Boletus, chanterelle, and oyster), cleaned and cut into large pieces or left whole

4 shallots, finely sliced (½ cup)

½ cup chopped herbs (mixture of fresh oregano, chives, and parsley)

½ teaspoon salt

½ teaspoon freshly ground black pepper

4 slices fine-textured white bread, each about 4 inches in diameter and ½ inch thick, crusts removed

Additional virgin olive oil, for garnish (optional)

Heat the butter and 1 tablespoon olive oil until very hot and hazelnut in color. Add the mushrooms and sauté over high heat for 10 seconds. Cover and continue cooking over high heat for 3 minutes. Uncover and cook over high heat for 2 to 3 minutes, until dry. Add the shallots, herbs, salt, and pepper, and cook for 1 minute longer.

Lightly toast the slices of bread and arrange them on a plate. Spoon the mushroom mixture on top of the toast, sprinkle a little olive oil on top, if desired, and serve immediately.

Yield: 4 servings

Nutritional analysis per serving: calories 195; protein 5 gm.; carbohydrates 22 gm.; fat 10.4 gm.; saturated fat 4.3 gm.; cholesterol 16 mg.; sodium 412 mg.

Tomatoes Stuffed with Yellow Grits

I prefer to use quick yellow grits, which have a coarser texture and are brighter yellow than cornmeal, in this lean recipe that is best made in full summer, when tomatoes are ripe, flavorful, and inexpensive. Although I use almost any leftovers—fish and meat, for example—to stuff tomatoes, this combination of grits, scallions, and mushrooms is perfect for a meatless lunch or dinner. The grits mixture can be served on its own, too, as a garnish or as a cushion under a piece of poached or grilled fish or sautéed meat.

1¼ teaspoons salt

½ cup quick yellow grits or yellow cornmeal

4 large, firm tomatoes (about 2 pounds)

3 tablespoons virgin olive oil

6 scallions, cleaned and cut into ½-inch pieces (1 cup)

1 medium onion (4 ounces), peeled and chopped (1 cup)

2 cloves garlic, chopped (1½ teaspoons)

½ pound mushrooms, coarsely chopped (2 cups)

Preheat the oven to 375 degrees. Bring 2½ cups water to a boil in a saucepan. Stir in ½ teaspoon of the salt and the grits, and return the mixture to a boil. Boil, covered, removing the lid and stirring with a whisk occasionally, for 15 minutes, until most of the water has been absorbed and the grits are tender. Spread the grits on a plate and cool them to lukewarm.

Meanwhile, remove a "cap" from the stem end of each tomato by cutting a ½-inch-thick slice crosswise from each. Reserve these "caps." Using a sharp-edged metal measuring tablespoon, remove the interior of the tomatoes, leaving a shell ½ inch thick. Chop the tomato insides in a food processor. (You should have 1½ to 2 cups.) Add ¼ teaspoon of the salt and 1 tablespoon of the olive oil, process briefly to mix, and set aside. This will be the sauce.

Heat the remaining 2 tablespoons of oil in a skillet until it is hot but not smoking. Add the scallions and onions, and sauté them over medium to high heat for 2 minutes. Stir in the garlic, the mushrooms, and the remaining ½ teaspoon of the salt. Cook for about 4 minutes longer, until most of the juices have evaporated. Transfer the mixture to a bowl and stir in the grits.

Fill the tomato shells with the grits mixture and top each with a "cap." Arrange the stuffed tomatoes in a gratin dish and pour the processed tomato sauce around them. Bake at 375 degrees for 40 minutes. Cool to lukewarm and serve.

Yield: 4 servings

Nutritional analysis per serving: calories 243; protein 6 gm.; carbohydrates 33 gm.; fat 11.4 gm.; saturated fat 1.5 gm.; cholesterol 0 mg.; sodium 713 mg.

Eggs in Aspic with Tarragon

Instead of using poached eggs in this recipe, I make *oeufs mollets*, preparing the eggs as if I were hard-cooking them, but removing them from the boiling water after only 4½ minutes. This brings the interior temperature of the eggs to about 140 or 150 degrees, which kills any salmonella bacteria that may be lurking there but leaves the yolk soft, like that of a poached egg. ❦ Eggs in aspic—*oeufs en gelée*—is a classic dish in French bourgeois cooking. In the summer, my family adores a good aspic, which means one made with a good stock. There is nothing more refreshing than eggs or fish, for example, served in a cold, flavorful *gelée*. Even though you may have avoided aspic dishes in the past, thinking them too sophisticated, try this one; it is stunningly beautiful and delicious. ❦ The clarification of the stock to make the aspic is a time-honored process and doesn't take long. Egg white is used as a coagulant to meld together all extraneous materials in the stock, making them easy to strain off. The result is a crystal-clear stock—free of fat and beautiful in color. The greens and peppercorns are used here the way you use tea: Steeping them in the boiling stock for a few minutes imparts flavor to the stock and lends substance to the clarification. Unflavored gelatin provides the texture needed to hold the stock together in an aspic.

4 small eggs

For clarified aspic

1 teaspoon salt, or to taste depending on the saltiness of the stock

1 egg white

2 cups greens (leaves of celery, leeks, parsley, and tarragon, and available herbs)

½ teaspoon black peppercorns, coarsely crushed (mignonnette)

2 envelopes (½ ounce each) unflavored gelatin (1½ tablespoons)

2½ cups good quality unsalted brown or white stock (preferably homemade), defatted

1 tablespoon coarsely chopped tarragon leaves

⅓ cup julienne strips of lean boiled ham (about 1½ ounces)

4 cups mixed salad greens, washed and dried

Toast

Prick the rounded end of each egg with a thumbtack to relieve pressure and keep the eggs from cracking when they are cooked. Bring 2 cups of water to a boil in a saucepan and gently lower the eggs into the water. Bring the water back to a boil and boil the eggs very gently for 4½ minutes. Then drain them and place them in a bowl of ice water.

When the eggs are completely cool, shell them carefully (preferably under cool running water, which makes the peeling easier and so helps protect the soft yolks inside), and return them to the cold water. Refrigerate until ready to use. (The recipe can be prepared to this point a few hours ahead.)

For the clarified aspic: Mix all the clarification ingredients except the stock in a large stainless steel saucepan. In another saucepan, bring the stock to a boil. Add about 1/3 cup of the boiling stock to the clarification mixture and mix well. Then add the rest of the stock, mix well, and place over high heat. Bring to a boil, mixing often to prevent the ingredients from sticking to the bottom of the pan and scorching. As soon as the mixture comes to a strong boil, reduce the heat to low and boil very gently for 4 minutes. *Do not disturb the mixture by stirring or shaking the pan.*

Remove the pan from the heat and let the mixture stand, undisturbed, for 10 minutes. Then strain it carefully through a strainer or colander lined with a paper or cloth towel. (You should have about 2 1/2 cups of very clean and clear liquid.)

Place about 2 tablespoons of the liquid aspic in each of four round or oval ramekins (3/4-cup capacity). When the aspic has set, sprinkle the tarragon and ham strips on top, dividing them among the four ramekins.

Remove the eggs from the cold water and pat them dry with paper towels. Place an egg in each of the ramekins. Cool the remainder of the aspic, and when it is cool but not yet set, spoon it around the eggs, filling up the ramekins. Refrigerate until set firm, about 2 hours.

To serve, arrange the mixed greens on a platter. Run a sharp knife around the edge of the ramekins to loosen the aspic and invert the molded eggs onto the greens. (Note: If unmolding is difficult, dip the bottoms of the ramekins into hot water for 4 to 5 seconds before unmolding.) Serve with toast.

Yield: 4 servings

Nutritional analysis per serving: calories 137; protein 16 gm.; carbohydrates 5 gm.; fat 6.2 gm.; saturated fat 1.8 gm.; cholesterol 218 mg.; sodium 757 mg.

Spinach, Ham, and Parmesan Soufflé

A soufflé is always an impressive addition to a meal. As a first course, this recipe will serve six generously, but it also makes a great luncheon main dish for four people. Although it can be prepared in a conventional soufflé mold, I like it best made in a gratin dish. The crust and topping, made of parmesan cheese and bread crumbs, will be browner and crunchier as a result, improving the look and taste of the dish and making it easier to serve at the table. ❦ I use spinach and ham in this dish, but you can eliminate the ham if you are cutting down on calories. Another green, or even mushrooms, can be substituted for the spinach.

10 ounces spinach, fibrous stems removed (8 ounces)

1 slice bread, processed in a food processor to make crumbs (½ cup)

½ cup freshly grated parmesan cheese

4 teaspoons unsalted butter

1 tablespoon canola oil

3 tablespoons all-purpose flour

1½ cups cold skim milk

¼ teaspoon salt

¼ teaspoon freshly ground black pepper

3 egg yolks

4 ounces lean ham, julienned (1 cup)

5 egg whites

Preheat the oven to 375 degrees. Wash the spinach and place it, still wet, in a skillet. Cook over medium to high heat for 2 minutes, until the spinach is wilted. Remove from the heat and cool. When it is cool, drain it, chop it coarsely, and set it aside.

Mix the bread crumbs and 3 tablespoons of the parmesan cheese together in a small bowl. Using 1 teaspoon of the butter, grease the sides and bottom of a 6-cup gratin dish that is about 1½ inches deep. Add half of the bread crumb and parmesan cheese mixture and shake the dish until the crumbs coat the sides and bottom. Set aside.

Melt the remaining 3 teaspoons of butter in a saucepan and add the oil and flour. Mix with a whisk and cook over medium to high heat for about 30 seconds. Whisk in the milk, salt, and pepper, and bring to a boil, whisking continuously until the mixture boils and thickens. Remove from the heat and whisk in the egg yolks. Add the reserved spinach and the ham, and mix well.

In a mixing bowl, beat the egg whites until they are firm but still soft. Fold them into the spinach mixture along with the remaining cheese.

Pour the soufflé mixture into the prepared gratin dish, sprinkle the remaining bread crumb and cheese mixture on top, place the dish on a tray, and bake it at 375 degrees for about 35 minutes, until the soufflé is set inside and the top is puffy and brown.

Spoon the soufflé directly from the gratin dish onto plates and serve immediately. (The soufflé can be unmolded from the dish by inverting it onto a plate, if you prefer to present it in this way.)

Note: If leftover soufflé is reheated in a conventional oven (preheated to 375 degrees) instead of a microwave oven, it will reinflate. Be sure to serve immediately.

Yield: 8 servings

Nutritional analysis per serving: calories 203; protein 15 gm.; carbohydrates 10 gm.; fat 11.2 gm.; saturated fat 4.5 gm.; cholesterol 130 mg.; sodium 641 mg.

Nage Courte of Striped Bass

S triped bass used to be almost impossible to find. Originally a sport fish, it became so scarce for a time that fishing for it was prohibited. Now striped bass of excellent quality are raised or "farmed" and available commercially in most parts of the country. If you can't find striped bass where you live, however, replace it with a fish of approximately the same size—anything from red snapper to porgy to black bass. ❦ I like to cook whole fish occasionally; the flesh slides off the bones easily and tends to have more flavor than when cooked as fillets. If you decide to prepare this recipe with fillets instead of whole fish, however, adjust the cooking time as indicated in the recipe.

1 leek (about 5 ounces), thoroughly cleaned and cut into julienne strips (about 2 cups)

1 large carrot (about 4 ounces), peeled and cut into julienne strips (about 1 cup)

4 strips lemon peel, removed with a vegetable peeler, stacked together, and cut into fine julienne strips (about 1½ tablespoons)

5 cloves garlic, peeled and sliced thin (1½ tablespoons)

1 small red onion, peeled and sliced thin (1 cup)

¾ cup dry white wine

1½ tablespoons virgin olive oil

1 tablespoon unsalted butter

1 teaspoon salt

2 whole striped bass, gutted, with heads removed (1¼ pounds each, ready to cook) or 4 fillets striped bass (about 6 ounces each) (if using fillets, see Note)

¼ teaspoon freshly ground black pepper

Place all the ingredients except the fish and pepper in a large stainless steel saucepan with ¾ cup water and bring to a boil over high heat. Cover, reduce the heat to medium, and boil gently for 2 minutes. Add the fish, bring to a boil, cover, reduce the heat to low, and cook for 5 minutes. Let the fish rest, covered, in the broth for 10 minutes before serving.

To serve, carefully remove the fish from the broth with a slotted spoon and place them on a clean work surface. Lift off the fillets, and remove and discard the skin. Transfer the fillets to four individual plates. Add the pepper to the stock and bring the mixture to a boil. Spoon the stock over the fish and serve immediately.

Note: If you are using fillets instead of whole fish, boil the vegetables for about 4 minutes before adding the fish. Place the fillets on top of the vegetables and bring the mixture to a boil. Cover and simmer for 1 minute, then set aside for 5 minutes. Serve the fillets with or without the skin, as desired.

Yield: 4 servings

Nutritional analysis per serving: calories 330; protein 32 gm.; carbohydrates 15 gm.; fat 12.1 gm.; saturated fat 3.3 gm.; cholesterol 144 mg.; sodium 694 mg.

Codfish in Olive and Horseradish Sauce

The pungent flavors of horseradish, capers, cilantro, and black olives dominate the codfish sauce. Even though the recipe contains sour cream, the dish is low-calorie, because it uses no oil or butter, the cod is a low-fat fish, and the sour cream amounts to only a tablespoon per person. If cod is not available, use fillets from another fleshy, white fish.

4 cod fillets, about 1½ inches thick (5 to 6 ounces each)

½ cup chopped onion

1 cup dry, fruity white wine (an Alsace wine would be good)

½ teaspoon salt

½ teaspoon freshly ground black pepper

About 12 oil-cured black olives

2 tablespoons small capers

2 tablespoons horseradish, freshly grated or bottled

¼ cup sour cream

4 tablespoons coarsely chopped cilantro (coriander or Chinese parsley)

Place the cod, onion, wine, salt, and pepper in a stainless steel saucepan. Bring to a boil over high heat, cover, reduce the heat to low, and boil gently for 2 minutes. (The cod will be undercooked at this point.) With a slotted spoon, carefully transfer the cod to a platter, cover it, and set it aside to continue cooking in its own residual heat.

Meanwhile, add the olives, capers, horseradish, and sour cream to the saucepan and bring to a boil. Arrange a cod fillet on each of four plates and top with the sauce. Sprinkle with the cilantro and serve immediately.

Yield: 4 servings

Nutritional analysis per serving: calories 234; protein 29 gm.; carbohydrates 4 gm.; fat 6.7 gm.; saturated fat 2.4 gm.; cholesterol 73 mg.; sodium 723 mg.

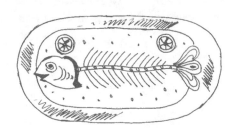

Christmas Oysters

I call these Christmas oysters (*huîtres de Noël*) because we like to serve oysters during the Christmas holidays and generally eat them as part of our Christmas dinner. We love oysters on the half shell, but at holiday time we like them served in this festive dish featuring a bright red pepper sauce and dark green spinach. ❦ *Hijiki* seaweed is already shredded and steamed, so it requires only soaking. My wife often makes an Oriental salad with *hijiki*, seasoning it with rice vinegar and a dash of sesame oil. If you can't find *hijiki* where you live, omit it as a garnish.

---

24 oysters, shucked, with juices and the deeper shell of each reserved (if desired for serving)

3 red bell peppers (1 pound), seeded and cut into 1-inch pieces

2 tablespoons unsalted butter

3/4 teaspoon salt

3 tablespoons virgin olive oil

3 to 4 cloves garlic, chopped (about 2 teaspoons)

1 pound spinach, washed, with tough stems removed and discarded (about 12 ounces)

1/4 teaspoon freshly ground black pepper

1/3 cup dried hijiki seaweed (available in Asian markets and many health food stores), soaked for 30 minutes in cold water and drained

Wash the shucked oysters in their own juices, lift them out, and place them in a stainless steel saucepan. Strain the oyster juices over the oysters. Set the pan aside.

For the red pepper sauce: Place the red peppers in a saucepan with 1/2 cup water. Bring to a boil, cover, and boil for 10 minutes. Remove the lid and continue cooking until the water has evaporated (about 5 minutes). Push the peppers through a food mill fitted with a fine screen. (You should have 1 1/4 cups.) Return to the saucepan and stir in 1 tablespoon of the butter and half of the salt. Set aside until serving time.

Heat 1 tablespoon of the oil in a skillet, add the garlic, and sauté for 10 seconds. Mix in the spinach and the remainder of the salt, and cook for 2 minutes, until the spinach is wilted and softened. Set aside off the heat.

At serving time, heat the oysters in their juices until barely boiling. (The oysters are cooked when the mantle or frill—the lacy collar all around the body—just begins to curl.) With a slotted spoon, transfer the oysters to a bowl and keep them warm.

For the oyster sauce: Bring the oyster juices to a strong boil. (You should have 2/3 cup. If you have more, boil until the juices are reduced to 2/3 cup; if less, add water to reach this amount.) Add the remaining tablespoon of butter, 2 tablespoons of oil, and the pepper. Bring back to a strong boil. Set aside momentarily while you prepare the plates.

To serve the oysters in their shells, arrange six of the reserved shells on each of four plates. Divide about 2 tablespoons of the red pepper sauce evenly among the shells on each plate. Place a rounded teaspoon of spinach on top of the sauce in each shell. Arrange an oyster on top of the spinach in each shell and spoon about a teaspoon of the oyster sauce on top of each oyster. Sprinkle with the *hijiki* and serve immediately.

To serve the oysters on plates, divide the red pepper sauce evenly among four plates and place a fourth of the spinach in the center of each plate. Arrange six oysters on top of the spinach on each plate and spoon 2 to 3 tablespoons of the oyster sauce over them. Sprinkle with the *hijiki* and serve immediately.

Yield: 4 servings

Nutritional analysis per serving: calories 251; protein 10 gm.; carbohydrates 14 gm.; fat 18.4 gm.; saturated fat 5.5 gm.; cholesterol 62 mg.; sodium 632 mg.

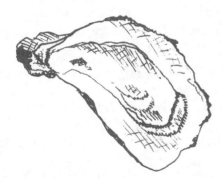

Cured Salmon in Molasses

his cured salmon recipe is interesting because the sweet molasses in combination with the dark soy sauce not only gives the salmon a very intense flavor but also colors the salmon flesh, making it almost black on the outside. When you slice it, the inside is a beautifully transparent gold and pink, contrasting dramatically with the black exterior and looking more like a smoked salmon, although no smoking is involved. ❦ This recipe is easy to do, but it takes time—the salmon is cured in the sugar, salt, and spices for 12 hours, then marinated in the molasses and sauce for another 24 hours, and finally set aside to dry for at least another 24 hours before it is sliced and served. When this much time is spent on a recipe, it makes sense to cure a large enough fillet so you have some on hand for entertaining. This recipe will serve eight. Any leftover salmon will keep for a week under refrigeration. You might enjoy serving it on salad greens, as suggested in the variation at the end of the recipe.

1 large salmon fillet (about 1½ pounds), preferably center cut, of even thickness throughout, with the skin left on but all bones removed

¼ cup coarse (kosher-style) salt

1 tablespoon sugar

1 teaspoon ground cumin

½ teaspoon ground allspice

½ teaspoon paprika

¼ teaspoon ground nutmeg

¼ teaspoon cayenne pepper

¼ cup dark molasses

2 tablespoons dark soy sauce

Buttered bread

For the optional garnishes

Chopped onion

Capers

Olive oil

Lightly score the skin of the salmon in a lattice pattern so the salt, sugar, and spices will penetrate through it to cure the flesh. (It is easier to cut through the skin if you hold the blade of the knife perpendicular to the fillet and run the entire length of the blade across the skin, instead of attempting to score it with just the tip of the blade.) Place the salmon in the center of a large piece of plastic wrap.

In a small bowl, mix together the salt, sugar, cumin, allspice, paprika, nutmeg, and cayenne. Spread the mixture evenly on both sides of the salmon and wrap the salmon tightly in the plastic wrap. Place it on a tray and refrigerate overnight or for at least 12 hours, to cure.

When ready to proceed, mix the molasses and soy sauce together in a small bowl. Unwrap the salmon, but don't remove it from the plastic wrap. Pour half of the molasses mixture over the top of the salmon and spread it evenly over the surface. Then turn the salmon over and coat the other side with the remainder of the molasses mixture. Rewrap the salmon in the plastic wrap, place it on the tray, and return it to the refrigerator for 24 hours.

Unwrap the salmon and remove it from the marinade. (It will have absorbed most of the marinade.) Discard any remaining marinade, pat the fish lightly with paper towels, and arrange it on a wire rack over a tray. Refrigerate it for another 24 hours to dry out.

At serving time, slice the salmon thinly on a slant and serve two or three slices per person with buttered bread. Garnish the salmon, if desired, with chopped onion, capers, and a drizzle of olive oil.

Yield: 8 servings

Nutritional analysis per serving: calories 146; protein 17 gm.; carbohydrates 6 gm.; fat 5.5 gm.; saturated fat 0.8 gm.; cholesterol 47 mg.; sodium 1,948 mg.

Recipe variation
Another way to serve the salmon

For a salad base for salmon slices

4 cups radicchio and Boston lettuce, mixed

1 tablespoon virgin olive oil

1½ teaspoons balsamic vinegar

⅛ teaspoon salt

¼ teaspoon freshly ground black pepper

8 to 12 thin slices Cured Salmon in Molasses

Toast

Wash the salad greens and dry them well. Combine the oil, vinegar, salt, and pepper in a bowl, add the greens, and toss gently to coat them with the dressing. Divide the greens among four serving plates, top each with 2 or 3 slices of salmon, and serve with toast.

Yield: 4 servings

Nutritional analysis per serving: calories 138; protein 12 gm.; carbohydrates 6 gm.; fat 7.2 gm.; saturated fat 1.0 gm.; cholesterol 31 mg.; sodium 1,374 mg.

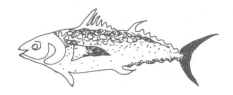

Salmon in Nori

My wife often makes sushi, and she always uses the dried seaweed sheets called *nori* for this. Made of dark green or purplish dried seaweed (*Porphyra tenera*), they measure about 7 by 8 inches and come sealed in plastic packages. They are available at some supermarkets and health food stores and at most Asian specialty shops. *Nori* sheets are flavorful and attractive, and Gloria's success with them spurred me to create this simple dish featuring salmon. ❦ *Nori* sheets are conventionally covered with cooked rice, which moistens them and thus makes them easy to roll. Here, I dampen one side of the *nori* with water before arranging pieces of salmon on top. The sheets soften immediately and the salmon can easily be rolled up in them and cut into pieces. These pieces are then steamed (I use a bamboo steamer), which takes only 5 minutes and is best done just before serving.

1 pound completely cleaned salmon, with a 4-by-8-inch piece of skin removed and reserved for crackling

Dash of salt

3 dried nori sheets

For the sauce

2 tablespoons canola oil

1½ teaspoons lemon juice

1 teaspoon julienne strips of lemon rind

1½ teaspoons balsamic vinegar

¼ teaspoon freshly ground black pepper

¼ teaspoon salt

Preheat the oven to 375 degrees. Spread the salmon skin on a cookie sheet, salt it lightly, and bake it at 375 degrees for 30 minutes, until crisp.

Meanwhile, cut the salmon into 3 strips, each about 1¼ inches wide and 7 inches long.

Wet the *nori* sheets on one side with water and place them, dampened side up, on a flat work surface. Place a strip of salmon at one end of each sheet and roll it tightly, enclosing the salmon. Cut each roll in half and then cut each half into thirds. You should have 6 slices per roll, or 18 slices in all, enough for 4 slices per person with a couple left over to pass around.

Arrange the *nori*-wrapped salmon pieces on a plate and place in a steamer over boiling water. Cover and steam for about 5 minutes, until the salmon is barely cooked, even slightly rare in the center.

Meanwhile, combine all the sauce ingredients in a small bowl.

Remove the salmon from the steamer and arrange it on a serving plate. Spoon some sauce over the salmon and sprinkle some salmon skin crackling on top. Serve.

Yield: 4 servings

Nutritional analysis per serving: calories 227; protein 23 gm.; carbohydrates 1 gm.; fat 14.0 gm.; saturated fat 1.6 gm.; cholesterol 62 mg.; sodium 243 mg.

You should have

fun in the kitchen and

then emerge from it

with flavorful,

wholesome, attractive

dishes that can be

served to both family

and guests.

Skate with Beets and Flavored Oil

kate, a relatively unknown fish in the United States, is quite common in Europe. Soft-fleshed, tender, moist, and mild-flavored, it is delicious. ❦ Conventionally, skate is poached, as it is here, in vinegar and water. Instead of serving it with butter, as is traditional, I coat it with a lower-calorie sauce featuring capers and garnish it with a julienne of beets seasoned with a fairly acidic dressing. In addition, for flavor and eye appeal, I surround the fish on each plate with some brilliant red beet-cooking liquid that I sprinkle with a little bright yellow Curried Oil (page 159) and vivid green Cilantro Oil (page 160).

For the beets and the skate

2 red beets (about 10 ounces total)

4 tablespoons red wine vinegar

¾ teaspoon salt

¼ teaspoon freshly ground black pepper

½ teaspoon sugar

1 large wing of peeled skate (about 1½ pounds)

For the caper sauce

3 tablespoons chopped red onion

2 tablespoons coarsely chopped scallions

1 tablespoons capers, drained

2 tablespoons Curried Oil (see page 159)

1 tablespoon red wine vinegar

¼ teaspoon salt

¼ teaspoon freshly ground black pepper

For the decorative oils

4 teaspoons Curried Oil (see page 159)

4 teaspoons Cilantro Oil (see page 160)

For the beets and the skate: Place the beets in a sauce-pan, cover them with cold water, and bring the water to a boil. Reduce the heat to low and boil gently, covered, for about 1 hour, until tender. Drain, reserving 1/3 cup of the cooking liquid. (Alternatively, place the beets in a bowl with 2 tablespoons of water. Cover with a glass lid and cook in a microwave oven until the beets are tender, about 30 minutes. There will be enough juice remaining around the beets for use around the fish.)

When the beets are cool enough to handle, peel them and cut them into thin (1/4-inch) julienne strips. Place the strips in the reserved cooking liquid and set aside.

Just before serving time, drain and reserve the beet liquid. To the beets add 1 tablespoon of the vinegar, 1/4 teaspoon of the salt, the pepper, and the sugar. Mix well.

Bring 6 cups water to a boil in a large saucepan. Stir in the remaining 3 tablespoons of vinegar and 1/2 teaspoon of salt. Add the skate, bring the mixture back to a boil, cover, reduce the heat to low, and boil gently for 15 minutes, while you make the sauce.

For the caper sauce: In a bowl combine all the sauce ingredients. Mix well and set aside.

To serve, arrange the beets on four plates. Remove the fish from the water, separate the flesh from the bones, and arrange equal amounts of fish on top of the beets. Cover with the caper sauce. Spoon about 1 1/2 tablespoons of the reserved beet juice around the fish on each plate and sprinkle 1 teaspoon of Curried Oil and then 1 teaspoon of Cilantro Oil on top of the beet juice. The blending of these liquids will create a beautiful design. Serve immediately.

Yield: 4 servings

Nutritional analysis per serving: calories 339; protein 38 gm.; carbohydrates 7 gm.; fat 17.2 gm.; saturated fat 2.0 gm.; cholesterol 94 mg.; sodium 759 mg.

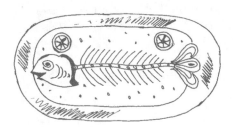

Scallops in Scallion Nests

This is an attractive, flavorful dish, ideal as the first course for an elegant dinner. The scallions, which are cooked briefly in boiling water and served with a mustard sauce, are good on their own—without the scallops—as a first course or salad. This same recipe is often done with leeks, but scallions work well, are less expensive, and can be found all year. ❦ I like this recipe made with large scallops. Cooked in a very hot skillet, they form a sweet brown crust on both sides. If you are using smaller scallops, cut the cooking time a little. The scallops should not be cooked until dry, but they shouldn't be flabby and soft inside either.

4 bunches small scallions (6 to 8 scallions per bunch)

For the mustard sauce

1 tablespoon Dijon-style mustard

1 tablespoon red wine vinegar

¼ cup virgin olive oil

¼ teaspoon salt

2 teaspoons cooking juices from the scallions

1 pound large scallops (about 12), washed

2 teaspoons virgin olive oil

⅛ teaspoon paprika

For the scallions: Cut off and discard the root ends of the scallions and about 2 inches of the green ends, along with any damaged leaves. Wash the scallions thoroughly.

Bring 1 cup water to a boil in a large stainless steel saucepan. Add the scallions, cover, and boil over high heat for 4 to 5 minutes, until tender. Remove the scallions with a slotted spoon (reserving any remaining cooking juices) and place them on a tray to cool. When they are cool, cover them with plastic wrap, and refrigerate them until serving time.

For the mustard sauce: In a small bowl, combine all the mustard sauce ingredients with a spoon. (Do not worry if the ingredients separate.)

For the scallops: Dry the scallops well with paper towels and place them in a bowl. Mix in the 2 teaspoons olive oil.

At serving time, heat a heavy saucepan or skillet (preferably cast iron) until very hot. Add the scallops and brown them for about 1 minute on each side. Set them aside off the heat to continue cooking in their own residual heat while you prepare the plates.

Reheat the scallions in a microwave oven for 20 to 30 seconds, just long enough to take the chill off. Arrange them on four plates, twisting them to form a circle or "nest" on the plate. Place 3 scallops in the center of each "nest" and coat with the mustard sauce. Sprinkle the paprika on top and serve immediately.

Yield: 4 servings

Nutritional analysis per serving: calories 276; protein 21 gm.; carbohydrates 11 gm.; fat 17.0 gm.; saturated fat 2.2 gm.; cholesterol 37 mg.; sodium 446 mg.

Scallop Seviche

T his interpretation of a South American dish is very flavorful and, since I make it without oil, quite lean. A mixture of hot pepper, cilantro, and mint gives it a hot, fresh taste that makes it a perfect entrée for a muggy summer day. The hotness of the dish can be increased or decreased depending on your tolerance for hot pepper.

1 pound sea scallops

1 small red onion, peeled and cut into ¼-inch pieces (1 cup)

1 ripe tomato (about 10 ounces), seeded and cut into ½-inch pieces (1½ cups)

3 tablespoons coarsely chopped cilantro (coriander or Chinese parsley)

2 tablespoons coarsely chopped mint

1 tablespoon finely julienned lime skin

Juice of 2 limes (about ¼ cup)

1 jalapeño pepper, seeded and chopped into fine dice (about 1 tablespoon; more or less can be used, depending on your tolerance for hotness)

1 teaspoon salt

½ teaspoon freshly ground black pepper

2 teaspoons sugar

2 tablespoons rice vinegar

1 small cucumber (8 ounces), trimmed and peeled

Remove and discard the muscles from the scallops, rinse them thoroughly, and cut them into ½-inch pieces or slices.

Combine all the ingredients except the cucumber in a plastic bag and refrigerate for at least 3 hours, turning the bag occasionally so the mixture is well combined.

Cut the cucumber in half lengthwise and scrape out the seeds with a sharp-edged metal measuring spoon. Then cut the cucumber halves lengthwise into about 24 strips and set them aside.

At serving time, make a decorative arrangement of 6 cucumber strips on each of four plates. Drain the seviche and spoon it on top of the cucumber strips. Serve.

Yield: 4 servings

Nutritional analysis per serving: calories 145; protein 21 gm.; carbohydrates 13 gm.; fat 1.2 gm.; saturated fat 0.1 gm.; cholesterol 37 mg.; sodium 609 mg.

Squid Salad à la Binh

My wife, Gloria, is addicted to this spicy squid salad inspired by a friend, Vietnamese chef and restaurateur, Binh Duong, who prepares a version of it frequently. There is no fat in the salad, and the only salt is in the *nuoc mam*, the traditional Vietnamese fish sauce, which is similar to sauces used in Thailand and the Philippines. ❦ I like hot peppers and use them generously here, but if you prefer your food less spicy, cut back on them. The salad is best made 24 hours ahead and will keep in the refrigerator for 4 or 5 days.

1 pound squid, pen removed and body thoroughly cleaned

4 cloves garlic, crushed and chopped fine (1 tablespoon)

2 to 3 small Thai hot peppers, seeded and chopped (about 1/2 teaspoon)

1 cup very thinly sliced onion

3 tablespoons lime juice

1/4 cup shredded fresh mint

1/4 cup shredded cilantro (coriander or Chinese parsley) leaves

2 tablespoons nuoc mam (fish sauce)

1/2 teaspoon sugar

1/4 teaspoon salt

4 large lettuce leaves

Bring 6 cups water to a boil in a large saucepan. Cut the body pieces of the squid crosswise into 1-inch slices and the tentacles into 1/2-inch pieces. Add the squid to the pot and cook for about 3 minutes, stirring occasionally, just until the water comes back to a boil. Drain immediately.

Meanwhile, combine the remaining ingredients except the lettuce in a serving bowl large enough to hold the squid. Add the hot, drained squid and toss until well mixed. Set aside for at least 10 minutes, stirring occasionally, so the dish can develop flavor.

Serve on the lettuce leaves.

Yield: 4 servings

Nutritional analysis per serving: calories 127; protein 16 gm.; carbohydrates 10 gm.; fat 2.2 gm.; saturated fat 0.5 gm.; cholesterol 206 mg.; sodium 179 mg.

Grilled Squid on Watercress

S quid is available almost everywhere now and usually comes cleaned in both fish stores and supermarkets. This makes it very easy to use. ❦ I like the chewy, rubbery texture of squid. It should not be overcooked or undercooked. To make it more flavorful when grilled, I blanch it briefly in boiling water (which tightens the skin and hardens the squid, so it can easily be impaled on skewers), and I season it lightly with olive oil and Italian seasoning. It is imperative that the grill be very hot and the rack clean so the squid is nicely marked but does not stick to the rack. ❦ Make certain that the watercress is well washed and thoroughly dried so there is no water to dilute the dressing. Toss the salad just before serving, since watercress greens wilt quickly.

1½ pounds cleaned, medium-size squid (about 16 pieces plus tentacles)

¼ teaspoon salt

¼ teaspoon freshly ground black pepper

2 tablespoons virgin olive oil

1 teaspoon Italian seasoning

1 large bunch watercress, stems removed and reserved for Watercress Soup (page 39), leaves thoroughly washed and dried

1 tablespoon peanut oil

1 teaspoon sherry vinegar

Dash of salt

Bring 6 cups water to a boil in a large saucepan. Drop the squid and tentacles into the boiling water and cook for 1 minute. (The water will not even return to the boil.) Drain the squid in a colander; their residual heat will help them dry.

After emptying out any water remaining in the bodies of the squid, arrange them in a dish and sprinkle them with the ¼ teaspoon salt, pepper, olive oil, and Italian seasoning.

Just before serving time, heat a grill until very hot. Toss the watercress with the peanut oil, sherry vinegar, and dash of salt. Arrange the salad on four plates.

Skewer the squid and tentacles, dividing them among 3 or 4 skewers, and cook them on the clean rack of the hot grill for 1½ minutes on each side.

Remove the squid and tentacles from the skewers and arrange about 4 squid per person with some of the tentacles on top of the watercress on each plate. Serve immediately.

Yield: 4 servings

Nutritional analysis per serving: calories 253; protein 28 gm.; carbohydrates 6 gm.; fat 12.5 gm.; saturated fat 2.1 gm.; cholesterol 397 mg.; sodium 265 mg.

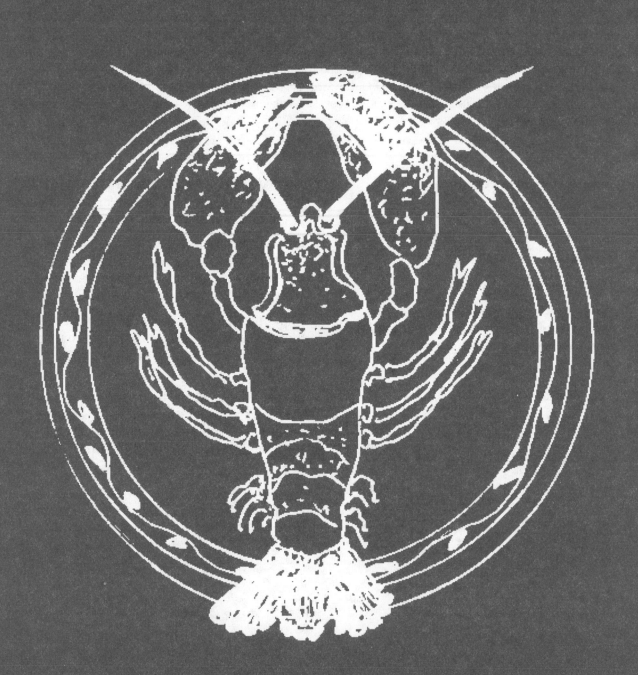

MAIN COURSES

Red Pepper Pasta with Walnuts, page 72

Risotto with Vegetables, page 74

Fines Herbes Omelets, page 75

Seafood with "Handkerchiefs," page 76

Lobster in Artichoke Bottoms, page 78

Grilled Salmon Fillets, page 80

Red Snapper in Brunoise Sauce, page 81

Tuna Steaks with Peppercorns, page 82

Chicken in Coriander Sauce, page 83

Chicken Supreme Kiev-Style, page 84

Poulet Rôti (Roasted Chicken), page 86

Stuffed and Roasted Cornish Hens, page 88

Turkey Fricadelles with Vegetable Sauce, page 90

Puerto Rican Pork and Beans, page 92

Fillet of Pork Charcutière, page 93

Slow-Cooked Pork Roast, page 94

Lamb Shanks and Beans Mulligan, page 95

Couscous of Lamb, page 96

Roasted Leg of Lamb, page 98

Veal Bitochki, page 99

Fricassee of Veal, page 100

Grilled Veal Chops with Caper Sauce, page 101

Breast of Veal Cocotte, page 102

Steak Maître d'Hôtel (Steak with Parsley Butter), page 103

Daube of Beef in Red Wine, page 104

Red Pepper Pasta with Walnuts

With its brilliant red color, this red pepper sauce has eye appeal as well as taste appeal. It is important to use a food mill here—if pureed in a food processor, the cooked red pepper must be strained afterward to remove the skin. The food mill does the pureeing and straining in one easy step. ❦ The pasta is seasoned after cooking with chopped onion, olive oil, parmesan cheese (optional), and parsley, and is flavorful enough to be served like this. The red pepper sauce enhances it greatly, however, making it an ideal meatless main dish for a summer dinner.

For the red pepper sauce

2 to 3 large red bell peppers (1½ pounds), seeded and cut into 1-inch pieces

5 cloves garlic, peeled

¾ teaspoon salt

¼ teaspoon freshly ground black pepper

3 tablespoons virgin olive oil

¾ pound linguini

1 tablespoon virgin olive oil

1 cup chopped onion

½ cup walnut pieces

½ teaspoon salt

¼ teaspoon freshly ground black pepper

2 tablespoons coarsely chopped parsley

2 to 3 tablespoons grated parmesan cheese (optional)

Bring 8 cups water to a boil in a large saucepan. Meanwhile, prepare the sauce.

For the red pepper sauce: Place the red pepper pieces in a saucepan with 1/2 cup water. Bring to a boil, cover, and boil gently for 10 minutes. Push the peppers and their cooking liquid through a food mill fitted with a fine screen. (You should have 1 3/4 cups.)

Crush the garlic with the flat side of a knife, chop it into a fine puree, and add it to the red pepper mixture with the 3/4 teaspoon salt, 1/4 teaspoon black pepper, and 3 tablespoons olive oil. Stir well with a whisk and set aside in the pan.

Add the linguini to the boiling water and cook it for about 8 minutes, until tender but still firm.

Meanwhile, heat the 1 tablespoon of olive oil in a skillet. When it is hot, add the onion and walnut pieces and sauté over medium heat for about 2 minutes, until the onion begins to brown. Transfer the mixture to the bowl in which you will serve the linguini, and stir in the 1/2 teaspoon salt, 1/4 teaspoon black pepper, and parsley.

Add 1/2 cup of the pasta-cooking liquid to the onions and walnuts in the bowl. Then drain the linguini in a colander.

Place the drained linguini in the serving bowl and mix well. Bring the red pepper sauce to a boil and divide it among four large plates. Mound the linguini in the center of each plate, sprinkle with the cheese, if desired, and serve immediately.

Yield: 4 servings

Nutritional analysis per serving: calories 591; protein 15 gm.; carbohydrates 80 gm.; fat 24.4 gm.; saturated fat 2.9 gm.; cholesterol 0 mg.; sodium 698 mg.

Risotto with Vegetables

Traditionally, risotto is made with more butter, oil, and cheese than I use here. For color, texture, and flavor, I incorporate vegetables in my version, and the resulting dish is almost a complete meal in itself. Although I serve this as a side dish, it would make a good meatless luncheon entrée or dinner first course. ❧ Regular canned chicken stock is often salty; if you use it instead of unsalted commercial or homemade stock, don't add as much salt as is called for here. Notice that I add more stock at the beginning of the cooking period because I know the rice will absorb at least this much liquid. Later, I add the remaining stock in smaller quantities, letting the rice absorb each addition before adding another and stopping when the rice is tender.

1 tablespoon unsalted butter

1 tablespoon virgin olive oil

¼ cup chopped onion

1 cup (8 ounces) arborio-type rice (small round-kerneled Italian rice)

About 3½ cups light, unsalted chicken stock (preferably homemade)

¾ teaspoon salt

For the vegetables

1 4-ounce piece fennel bulb, coarsely chopped (⅔ cup)

4 asparagus spears (about 4 ounces total), peeled and cut into ½-inch pieces (1 cup)

1 cup frozen petite peas

1 small red pepper (4 ounces), peeled and cut into ¼-inch pieces (1 cup)

3 large mushrooms (3 ounces), cut into ¼-inch julienne strips (1 cup)

¼ cup grated parmesan cheese

Heat the butter and oil in a skillet. When they are hot, add the onion and sauté for 1 minute. Add the rice, mix well, and stir in 2½ cups of the stock. Cook for 12 minutes, covered, over medium heat, removing the lid two or three times to stir the rice, which otherwise tends to stick to the bottom of the pan. Then uncover the pan and continue cooking the rice, stirring occasionally, until all the stock has been absorbed.

Add the fennel to the pan with another ½ cup of the stock and cook, covered, for 5 minutes, removing the lid once or twice to stir the rice.

Add the remainder of the vegetables, stock, and salt, and cook, uncovered, another 5 minutes, stirring, until the mixture is creamy and the rice is tender. Stir in the cheese and serve immediately.

Yield: 4 servings

Nutritional analysis per serving: calories 368; protein 12 gm.; carbohydrates 57 gm.; fat 10.0 gm.; saturated fat 3.9 gm.; cholesterol 13 mg.; sodium 664 mg.

Fines Herbes Omelets

The *fines herbes* omelet is my favorite; it reminds me somehow of spring, the time of year when fresh herbs begin to appear. Tarragon, chives, and chervil are strongly scented and wonderfully flavorful. Even though we don't eat as many eggs as we once did, they make a nice occasional replacement for meat or fish. One of my favorite family dinner menus includes this omelet, Salad with *Saucisson* (page 44), and Potato Sauté *à Cru* (page 115). ❦ The mixture of herbs I use here—parsley, tarragon, chives, and chervil—is the classic combination for a *fines herbes* omelet, but you can replace some or all of these with other fresh herbs. ❦ Use good quality eggs for this dish, purchasing them, if possible, from an organic farm, where the chickens range free to feed on pesticide-free, insecticide-free grass and natural grains.

10 large eggs

½ teaspoon freshly ground black pepper

¼ teaspoon salt

½ cup loosely packed chopped herbs (a mixture of ¼ cup chopped parsley and ¼ cup combined tarragon, chives, and chervil)

2 teaspoons canola oil

2 teaspoons unsalted butter

Using a fork, beat the eggs, pepper, and salt in a bowl until thoroughly mixed and well combined. Stir in the herbs.

Heat 1 teaspoon each of the oil and butter in a 10-inch nonstick omelet pan over high heat. When the oil and butter are hot, add half the egg mixture. Stir it continuously with a fork while shaking the pan for about 2 minutes to create the smallest possible curds. When most of the mixture is solid, cook it without stirring for 10 seconds to create a thin "skin" on the underside of the mixture, binding it together.

Roll the omelet by bringing together two of its edges from opposite sides of the pan. Invert it onto a plate and repeat the process, using the remainder of the ingredients to create a second omelet. Serve immediately, half an omelet per person.

Yield: 2 omelets, 4 servings

Nutritional analysis per serving: calories 227; protein 16 gm.; carbohydrates 2 gm.; fat 16.7 gm.; saturated fat 5.2 gm.; cholesterol 536 mg.; sodium 295 mg.

Seafood with "Handkerchiefs"

This savory recipe looks more complicated to make than it is. Egg roll wrappers, available packaged at most supermarkets, are pliable enough to roll easily when lightly oiled. Watercress leaves, sandwiched between two wrappers, are visible through the almost transparent surface of the cooked wrappers. Served on top of the seafood, they make a beautiful presentation, looking somewhat like a casually dropped handkerchief. ❦ While I use oysters, scallops, and salmon in this recipe, either the oysters or the scallops could be replaced by another shellfish, such as shrimp, and another fish could be substituted for the salmon. If oysters are not used, replace their juice with 1/4 cup each water and dry white wine.

8 egg roll wrappers, each 6 inches square

Canola oil for coating "handkerchiefs"

16 leaves watercress

12 unshelled oysters

1 yellow pepper (8 ounces), peeled and cut into julienne strips (about 1 cup)

2 tablespoons chopped scallions

2 tablespoons olive oil

1 tablespoon unsalted butter

1/2 teaspoon salt

1/4 teaspoon freshly ground black pepper

1/2 pound bay scallops

1/2 pound salmon, cleaned and cut into 1-inch pieces

Bring about 1 1/2 quarts water to a boil in a medium-size saucepan.

Meanwhile, lightly oil a flat, nonporous surface (such as marble or Formica), place an egg roll wrapper on it, and arrange 4 watercress leaves randomly on top. Lightly dampen a second wrapper on one side with water and press it, dampened side down, on top of the first wrapper, creating a "sandwich" with the watercress inside. Lightly oil the top of the "sandwich" and roll it with a rolling pin to create an 8-inch-square "handkerchief." Make 3 additional "handkerchiefs" with the remaining wrappers and watercress leaves.

Poach the "handkerchiefs" one at a time, dropping them into the boiling water and cooking them for 1 1/2 minutes each. Remove them with a slotted spoon and transfer each "handkerchief" as it is cooked to a bowl of cold water. Set aside.

Wash the oysters under cold water and shuck them over a bowl to catch the juices. (You should have 1/3 to 1/2 cup juice.) Set the oysters aside in another bowl.

Allow the oyster juices to sit undisturbed for a few minutes and then carefully pour them into a saucepan, leaving behind any sandy residue that may have settled to the bottom of the bowl. Add the yellow pepper, scallions, olive oil, butter, salt, and pepper to the saucepan, bring the mixture to a boil, and boil for 30 seconds. Add the scallops and salmon, and return the mixture to a boil. Stir. Add the oysters, return the mixture to a boil, stir again, and remove immediately from the heat.

Meanwhile, bring a pot of water to a boil. Lift the egg roll "handkerchiefs" from the cold water and plunge them into the boiling water for about 10 seconds to reheat them.
Divide the seafood mixture evenly among four plates and arrange a hot "handkerchief" decoratively on top of each serving. Serve immediately.

Yield: 4 servings

Nutritional analysis per serving: calories 453; protein 30 gm.; carbohydrates 36 gm.; fat 20.5 gm.; saturated fat 4.0 gm.; cholesterol 120 mg.; sodium 454 mg.

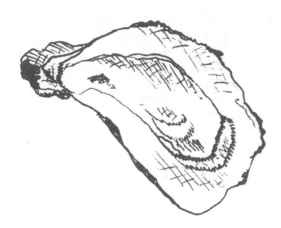

Lobster in Artichoke Bottoms

Lobster and artichokes are two of my favorite foods, and I combine them here in a great entrée for an elegant meal. ❦ It is always a problem to serve whole lobsters; they are messy to eat, and much of the meat is wasted because people don't know how to remove it from the shells. Instead, cook the lobsters and extract the meat ahead. Then serve it as I do here in tender artichoke bottoms with a light sauce made from the lobster stock. Leftover stock is also good as the base for a bisque, or you can add pasta and seasonings to it for a simple and delicious soup (see Lobster Broth with Pasta, page 18).

2 lobsters (about 1½ pounds each)

For the artichoke bottoms

4 medium artichokes (about 2 pounds total), leaves and bases trimmed to make artichoke bottoms

1 tablespoon virgin olive oil

1½ teaspoons lemon juice

¼ teaspoon salt

2 tablespoons unsalted butter

2 tablespoons minced chives

Salt and freshly ground black pepper to taste

Bring 2 quarts water to a boil in a large kettle. Add the lobsters, bring the water back to a boil, cover, reduce the heat to low, and boil the lobsters gently for 15 minutes. Lift the lobsters from the cooking liquid and set them aside until cool enough to handle. Then remove the meat from the shells and reserve it, along with the red roe. (You should have about ¾ pound of meat.) Cut the meat of each tail in half lengthwise, and discard any remaining intestinal tract.

Place the shells back in the kettle with the cooking liquid and boil, covered, for 30 minutes. Strain. (You should have about 7 cups of stock.) Set 1 cup of stock aside for the sauce and freeze the remainder for use in a bisque or for serving with pasta (see Lobster Broth with Pasta, page 18).

For the artichoke bottoms: Place the artichoke bottoms in a saucepan with 1 cup water, the oil, lemon juice, and salt. Bring to a boil, cover, reduce the heat, and boil the artichokes gently for about 20 minutes, until they are tender and most of the cooking liquid has evaporated. Let cool. When the artichokes are cool enough to handle, remove and discard the chokes.

Just before serving time, reheat the artichoke bottoms for about 1 minute in a microwave oven or for 10 to 15 minutes in a conventional oven set at 350 degrees. Place the roe in an ovenproof dish and heat it for 5 minutes in a 350-degree oven to dry it. Chop the roe coarsely with a knife.

Reheat the lobster meat for 20 to 30 seconds in a microwave oven or for 8 to 10 minutes in a conventional oven set at 350 degrees. Bring the cup of reserved stock to a boil and boil it until it is reduced to 1/2 cup. Add the butter, chives, and salt and pepper to taste, and bring to a strong boil.

Arrange an artichoke bottom on each of four plates and place the meat of half a lobster tail in the cavity of each with a piece of claw meat alongside. Spoon some sauce on top and sprinkle with some of the roe. Serve, if desired, with Broccoli with Butter, page 109, arranging the broccoli around the artichoke bottoms.

Yield: 4 servings

Nutritional analysis per serving: calories 208; protein 21 gm.; carbohydrates 11 gm.; fat 9.7 gm.; saturated fat 4.1 gm.; cholesterol 77 mg.; sodium 577 mg.

Grilled Salmon Fillets

Salmon is available throughout the country now and can usually be found fresh. Grilling is one of the best ways to cook salmon, although if this is not an option for you, you can cook it in a skillet. I have included directions for this in the note at the end of the recipe. ❦ The success of this dish depends on the use of unskinned salmon fillets. The skin must be scaled first, so ask your fish market to do this when you buy the salmon, or do it yourself. I cook the fillets skin side down, which makes the skin appealingly crisp and protects the flesh at the same time, keeping it moist. You'll notice that I cook the salmon for only a few minutes; my family prefers it slightly rare.

4 pieces (6 to 7 ounces each, about 1 inch thick) boneless salmon fillets with the skin on, scaled

¼ teaspoon salt

1 teaspoon corn or canola oil

1 piece (4 to 6 inches) Japanese daikon radish

4 teaspoons virgin olive oil (optional)

Additional oil (optional) for sprinkling on salmon before serving

Preheat the oven to 180 degrees. Heat a grill (preferably one with a lid) until it is very hot. Sprinkle the fleshy inside of the salmon fillets with the salt and pat the skin side with the oil.

Place the salmon, skin side down, on a clean rack on the very hot grill and cover with the lid. Cook over high heat for about 2 minutes for 1-inch-thick steaks that are light pink and slightly underdone inside. (Decrease or increase the cooking time based on the thickness of your fillets and your taste preferences.)

When the salmon is cooked to your liking, place it, skin side up, in a nonstick ovenproof skillet and place the skillet in a 180-degree oven for a few minutes while you finish the

dish. The salmon will continue to cook in its own residual heat.

With a vegetable peeler, peel the outer skin of the daikon radish. Then cut the radish into strips, stack the strips, and cut them into a fine julienne.

To serve, arrange the salmon, skin side up, on individual plates and sprinkle the julienne of radish on top. If desired, serve with Ragout of Asparagus (page 108) and Grilled Portobello Mushrooms (page 111). If the salmon is eaten on its own, sprinkle each fillet with 1 teaspoon of oil, if desired, just before serving.

Note: If you do not have a grill, heat a sturdy cast iron or heavy aluminum skillet for 2 to 3 minutes over high heat. Add the salmon fillets, skin side down, and cook them, covered, for 2 minutes (slightly longer or less, as you prefer, for the thickness of your fillets). Set aside, covered, for 2 or 3 minutes and serve while the salmon is still slightly pink inside.

Yield: 4 servings

Nutritional analysis per serving: calories 276; protein 37 gm.; carbohydrates 1 gm.; fat 12.8 gm.; saturated fat 1.9 gm.; cholesterol 101 mg.; sodium 221 mg.

Red Snapper in Brunoise Sauce

I use red snapper fillets here, but the recipe can be prepared with fillets from any fresh, firm-fleshed fish. The cooking time is based on the thickness of the fillets, so make appropriate adjustments if your fillets are thicker or thinner than mine. ❦ This is an easy, quick recipe. First, all the ingredients but the snapper are cooked together for a few minutes in a skillet. At serving time, the fish is added, cooked for a couple of minutes, and then served with a sauce created from the mixture in the pan.

1 small leek, washed and finely sliced (1½ cups)

3 ounces mushrooms, washed and cut into julienne strips (1½ cups)

¼ cup chopped shallots

⅓ cup peeled (with a vegetable peeler), diced (¼-inch dice) red bell pepper

1 cup dry white wine

2 tablespoons virgin olive oil

½ teaspoon salt

¼ teaspoon freshly ground black pepper

4 red snapper fillets, about 5 ounces each, boneless but with skin on

1 tablespoon unsalted butter

Place all the ingredients except the fish and butter in a stainless steel saucepan. Cover, bring to a boil, reduce the heat to low, and boil gently for 3 minutes. Add the fish, cover, and cook for 2½ to 3 minutes for fillets that are about ¾ inch thick. (Increase or decrease the cooking time proportionately for fillets of different thicknesses.)

Arrange a fillet on each of four plates. Add the butter to the drippings in the saucepan and bring the mixture to a strong boil. Divide the mixture among the plates, spooning both sauce and vegetables on top of the fish. Serve immediately.

Yield: 4 servings

Nutritional analysis per serving: calories 306; protein 31 gm.; carbohydrates 9 gm.; fat 11.7 gm.; saturated fat 3.1 gm.; cholesterol 60 mg.; sodium 378 mg.

Tuna Steaks with Peppercorns

Tuna is an ideal replacement here for beef, the classic choice in pepper steak recipes. Thick tuna steaks are wonderfully moist and flavorful prepared this way and served rare. ❦ I use a mixture of four different peppercorns: mild, brown-speckled Szechuan peppercorns; black peppercorns; white peppercorns, which are the same berry as the black but with the skin removed; and Jamaican peppercorns, better known as allspice. One or another of these varieties can be omitted if not available, and the total amount of pepper used can be adjusted to accommodate your taste preferences, although cracked pepper used in this way is much milder than you might imagine.

1 teaspoon Szechuan peppercorns

1/2 teaspoon white peppercorns

1/2 teaspoon black peppercorns

1 teaspoon allspice berries (Jamaican peppercorns)

4 tuna steaks 1 inch thick (about 6 ounces each)

1 tablespoon corn oil

1/2 teaspoon salt

Crush the peppercorns with a meat pounder or the bottom of a saucepan. Brush both sides of the steaks with the oil and then sprinkle both sides with the salt and crushed pepper.

Heat a cast iron pan for 2 to 3 minutes, until very hot. Place the steaks in the pan and cook them over very high heat for about 1 1/2 minutes on each side. Cover the pan, remove from the heat, and let stand for 3 to 5 minutes before serving. The steaks will continue to cook in their own residual heat but should remain pink inside.

Yield: 4 servings

Nutritional analysis per serving: calories 278; protein 40 gm.; carbohydrates 1 gm.; fat 11.8 gm.; saturated fat 2.6 gm.; cholesterol 65 mg.; sodium 340 mg.

Chicken in Coriander Sauce

I use only chicken thighs here and generously serve two per person. Make sure that you have a large nonstick skillet or saucepan for this recipe, because you'll remove the skin from the chicken and the pieces tend to stick when sautéed skinless in a conventional pan. ❦ My family loves the taste of coriander, but, if you object to its distinctive flavor, use parsley or another herb more to your liking.

1½ teaspoons corn oil

8 chicken thighs (about 3 pounds total), skin and visible fat removed (2¼ pounds trimmed)

¾ pound onions, peeled and sliced thin (4 cups)

8 cloves garlic, peeled and sliced thin (3 tablespoons)

½ cup dry white wine

1 small bunch cilantro (coriander or Chinese parsley), stems removed and finely chopped (2 tablespoons) and leaves coarsely chopped (¼ cup loosely packed)

½ teaspoon salt

½ teaspoon freshly ground black pepper

Heat the oil in a large nonstick skillet. When it is hot, add the thighs in one layer and sauté them over medium to high heat for 4 minutes on each side, until nicely browned.

Remove the chicken to a platter. Add the onions to the drippings in the skillet. Sauté for 1 minute. Stir in the garlic, wine, and coriander stems, and sauté for 10 seconds longer. Return the chicken to the skillet, add the salt and pepper, and bring the surrounding liquid to a boil. Cover the pan, reduce the heat, and boil gently for 15 minutes.

Stir in the coriander leaves and serve two chicken thighs per person.

Yield: 4 servings

Nutritional analysis per serving: calories 308; protein 40 gm.; carbohydrates 10 gm.; fat 9.4 gm.; saturated fat 2.2 gm.; cholesterol 161 mg.; sodium 446 mg.

Chicken Supreme Kiev-Style

I call this Kiev-style chicken to differentiate it from the famous Chicken Kiev that inspired it. In the original recipe, the chicken is usually left unskinned, stuffed with butter, dipped in eggs and bread crumbs, and then deep-fried—setting it a world apart from my rendition. I use skinless chicken, stuff it with a mushroom puree, and roll it in fresh bread crumbs that are seasoned with herbs and only moistened with oil. Much lower in calories, my version is intensely flavored, moist, and delicious.

4 boneless chicken breasts (about 7 ounces each), with skin and any visible fat removed

For the mushroom filling

1½ tablespoons virgin olive oil

1½ cups chopped onions

8 ounces mushrooms, cleaned and chopped (3 cups)

3 to 4 cloves garlic, peeled, crushed, and chopped (1 tablespoon)

½ teaspoon salt

¼ teaspoon freshly ground black pepper

2 tablespoons coarsely chopped cilantro (coriander or Chinese parsley)

For the coating

4 slices firm white bread, processed in a food processor to make crumbs (2 cups)

2 tablespoons virgin olive oil

2 tablespoons chopped cilantro

½ teaspoon salt

½ teaspoon freshly ground black pepper

¼ cup skim milk

Preheat the oven to 400 degrees. Butterfly the chicken breasts: Holding your knife so the blade is parallel to the cutting surface, slice almost all the way through the thickness of each breast, stopping when you can open the breast as you would a book and lay the attached halves flat. Pound the breasts lightly, and set them aside while you make the filling.

For the filling: Heat the olive oil in a large skillet. When it is hot, add the onions and sauté over medium to high heat for about 2 minutes. Stir in the mushrooms, garlic, salt, and pepper, and cook, covered, for about 3 minutes. Remove the lid and continue cooking until there is no visible liquid remaining in the skillet. Add the cilantro and transfer the mixture to a plate to cool.

When the filling is cool, divide it into four equal portions and mound one portion in the center of each butterflied chicken breast. Fold all edges of the breast meat over the filling to enclose it completely.

For the coating: Combine the bread crumbs, oil, cilantro, salt, and pepper together in a bowl. Dip the stuffed chicken breasts in the milk and then roll them in the seasoned bread crumbs.

Arrange the coated chicken breasts in a roasting pan and bake them at 400 degrees for 20 to 25 minutes, until cooked through but still moist. Serve immediately with Bulgur Wheat Pilaf, page 123.

Yield: 4 servings

Nutritional analysis per serving: calories 391; protein 42 gm.; carbohydrates 21 gm.; fat 15 gm.; saturated fat 2.4 gm.; cholesterol 95 mg.; sodium 776 mg.

Poulet Rôti

Roasted Chicken

This classic way to cook chicken is still the simplest and best method. Roasting the bird at a high temperature crystallizes the skin, making it delectably crisp, and this skin protects the flesh, keeping it moist. ❦ The skin can be removed and discarded at the end of the cooking period, if you want the dish to be less caloric. From a health standpoint, it is essential that you discard almost all the fat that has accumulated around the chicken during the cooking process, retaining only enough to season the *Coquillettes au Gruyère*, should you elect to serve them with the chicken. The solidified juice that remains after the fat is skimmed off becomes a flavorful sauce for the chicken. ❦ For best results, do not cover the chicken while it is roasting; if covered with a piece of aluminum foil, for example, it will start steaming and taste reheated when served. For maximum flavor, the chicken should be served no more than 45 minutes after roasting.

---

1 chicken (about 3½ pounds)

¼ teaspoon salt

¼ teaspoon freshly ground black pepper

1 teaspoon virgin olive oil

1 recipe Coquillettes au Gruyère (page 122), with variations indicated below (optional)

1 bunch watercress, for garnish

Preheat the oven to 425 degrees. Sprinkle the chicken inside and out with the salt and pepper. Truss the chicken if you like, although this is not required. Heat the oil in a large ovenproof nonstick skillet until it is hot but not smoking. Place the chicken on its side in the skillet and brown it over medium to high heat for about 2½ minutes. Then turn the chicken over and brown it on the other side for 2½ minutes.

Place the skillet, with the chicken still on its side, in the 425-degree oven. Roast it, uncovered, for 20 minutes. Then turn the chicken onto its other side and roast it for another 20 minutes. Finally, turn the chicken onto its back, baste it with the fat that has emerged during the cooking, and roast it, breast side up, for 10 minutes.

Remove the chicken from the oven and place it, breast side down, on a platter. Pour the drippings from the skillet into a bowl and set them aside for a few minutes to allow the fat to rise to the top.

To serve, carve the chicken, separating the legs from the thighs and cutting each breast in half. Arrange a piece of dark meat and a piece of white meat on each of four plates.

If you are *not* serving the *Coquillettes au Gruyère* (Pasta Shells with Swiss Cheese) (see page 122) with the chicken, deglaze the skillet by adding 2 to 3 tablespoons water and stirring to loosen and melt any solidified juices. Add to the drippings in the bowl. Skim off and discard most of the fat from the reserved drippings and serve the defatted drippings with the chicken, garnishing each serving with a few sprigs of watercress.

If you *are* serving *Coquillettes au Gruyère,* bring 2 quarts water to a boil in a large saucepan and cook the pasta as directed in the recipe on page 122. Place the 1/2 cup of reserved pasta-cooking liquid in the unwashed skillet used to cook the chicken. Bring to a boil, stirring to release and dissolve any solidified juices in the skillet, and place this deglazing liquid in a bowl large enough to hold the pasta.

Skim off about 3 tablespoons of clear fat that has risen to the top of the bowl of reserved chicken drippings and add those tablespoons to the deglazing liquid in the large bowl. Remove and discard any remaining surface fat from the drippings and add the defatted drippings to the large bowl. Add the pasta and complete the recipe as indicated on page 122. Serve immediately with the chicken.

Yield: 4 servings

Nutritional analysis per serving: calories 428; protein 48 gm.; carbohydrates 0.1 gm.; fat 24.9 gm.; saturated fat 6.8 gm.; cholesterol 154 mg.; sodium 279 mg.

Stuffed and Roasted Cornish Hens

Little Cornish hens are quite flavorful prepared this way, and two, weighing only a pound and a quarter each, are sufficient for four people with the bulgur wheat stuffing. ❧ For an even leaner presentation, you can remove the skin from the hens before serving them. However, the hens are cooked at such a high temperature that most of the fat in the skin emerges and collects in the bottom of the roasting pan. You discard this liquid fat at the end of the cooking period and combine the remaining drippings with a little water to form a natural juice that is delicious with the hens. ❧ Try to buy your bulgur wheat in a health food store, where it is usually much less expensive and better in quality than that sold elsewhere. Be sure to buy true bulgur, not just cracked wheat. The latter is uncooked; the former is cracked wheat that has been steamed and dried; it needs only to be reconstituted in water.

⅓ cup bulgur wheat

2 Cornish hens, about 1¼ pounds each

4 teaspoons canola oil

1 leek (4 ounces), roots and damaged or wilted leaves removed, remainder chopped (1¼ cups)

1 onion (3 ounces), chopped (about ¾ cup)

2 cloves garlic, peeled, crushed, and chopped (about 1½ teaspoons)

1 teaspoon chopped jalapeño pepper (more or less depending on your tolerance for hotness)

1 Granny Smith apple (7 ounces), cored and cut (unpeeled) into ⅜-inch pieces (about 1¼ cups)

¼ teaspoon freshly ground black pepper

½ teaspoon salt

Bring 1 cup water to a boil in a saucepan, stir in the bulgur wheat, and set the pan aside off the heat for 1 hour. Drain. (You should have 1 cup.)

Preheat the oven to 425 degrees. Bone the Cornish hens from the neck opening without tearing the skin. Reserve the bones to make stock or soup at another time.

Heat 3 teaspoons of the canola oil in a large skillet. When it is hot, add the leek and onion, and sauté for 2 to 3 minutes, until the vegetables are wilted and translucent. Add the garlic and jalapeño, and mix well. Stir in the apple, black pepper, three-fourths of the salt, and the bulgur. Mix well and cook, uncovered, over medium heat for 2 to 3 minutes, until any additional moisture in the wheat is absorbed and it is fluffy. Cool.

Stuff the boned hens with the cooled apple and wheat mixture, and tie the hens with twine to enclose the stuffing.

Spread the remaining teaspoon of oil in the bottom of a small roasting pan. Place the hens in the pan and sprinkle them with the remaining salt. Roast them at 425 degrees for 40 minutes, basting the hens with the juices and fat that emerge from them after 15 minutes and again after 30 minutes.

Remove the hens to a platter. Pour out and discard any fat that has accumulated in the roasting pan. Add ½ cup water to the pan and bring it to a boil, stirring to release and melt the solidified juices in the pan.

Cut the hens in half, remove the twine, divide the juice among four plates, and place half a hen on each plate. Serve immediately.

Yield: 4 servings

Nutritional analysis per serving: calories 435; protein 36 gm.; carbohydrates 23 gm.; fat 21.9 gm.; saturated fat 5.1 gm.; cholesterol 110 mg.; sodium 385 mg.

Turkey Fricadelles with Vegetable Sauce

T his is my variation of a dish that my wife prepares occasionally. I make a mousse with very lean ground turkey meat, an egg, and ice cubes (which make the meat sufficiently spongy and juicy). Then, I quickly mix in some blanched vegetables for color and texture, and form the mixture into patties. Served with a mushroom and tomato sauce, the *fricadelles* are tasty, attractive, and very low in calories.

1 cup shredded or finely sliced carrot (2 ounces)

3 cups (lightly packed) spinach leaves, cleaned (3 ounces)

1 pound ground raw turkey meat

⅓ cup small ice cubes

1 egg

¾ teaspoon salt

½ teaspoon freshly ground black pepper

For the vegetable sauce

1 tablespoon virgin olive oil

¼ cup chopped onion

4 ounces mushrooms, cut into ¼-inch pieces (1½ cups)

12 ounces tomatoes, cut into ½-inch pieces (2½ cups)

3 cloves garlic, peeled, crushed, and chopped (2 teaspoons)

½ teaspoon salt

1 tablespoon canola oil

Bring ½ cup water to a boil in a saucepan. Add the carrot and cook for 1 minute. Then, add the spinach and cook for 1 minute. Drain, reserving the cooking liquid (you should have ½ cup) for use in the sauce, and cool the vegetables.

Place the turkey meat, ice, and egg in the bowl of a food processor and process for 20 seconds, scraping down the sides of the bowl after 10 seconds. Add the salt, pepper, carrots, and spinach, and process for about 5 seconds. Transfer the mixture to a bowl and form it into four equal patties. Wrap the patties in plastic wrap and refrigerate them while you make the sauce.

For the vegetable sauce: Heat the olive oil in a skillet. When it is hot but not smoking, sauté the onion over medium to high heat for 1 minute. Add the mushrooms, cook for 2 minutes, and then add the tomatoes, garlic, and salt along with the reserved ½ cup vegetable cooking liquid. Bring the mixture to a boil, cover, reduce the heat to low, and cook for 5 minutes.

About 15 minutes before serving time, heat the canola oil over medium heat in a nonstick skillet large enough to hold the turkey patties in one layer. When the oil is hot, add the patties and cook them, uncovered, for 3 minutes on one side. Turn them over and cook them, covered, for 3 minutes on the other side. Discard the fat and set the patties aside to rest, covered, in the skillet for 5 minutes before serving.

Serve one patty per person with some sauce.

Yield: 4 servings

Nutritional analysis per serving: calories 311; protein 24 gm.; carbohydrates 9 gm.; fat 19.9 gm.; saturated fat 4.2 gm.; cholesterol 110 mg.; sodium 801 mg.

Puerto Rican Pork and Beans

My wife, Gloria, is of Puerto Rican ancestry, and she often prepares this type of dish when we have guests, especially family visiting from Europe. A satisfying, one-dish meal, it can be cooked ahead and frozen, and it is even better reheated. ❦ Buy the meatiest, leanest country-style spareribs you can find. Note that the cilantro stems are cooked with the beans to give them an unusual and definitive flavor, and then the leaves are added at the end. We particularly like the flavor of cilantro, but if you object to its taste, omit it from the recipe.

1 tablespoon canola oil

4 country-style pork loin spareribs (about 1½ pounds)

1 medium carrot, peeled and cut into ½-inch cubes (about ½ cup)

2 medium onions (about 10 ounces total), peeled and cut into ½-inch cubes (½ cup)

6 cloves garlic, peeled and chopped (about 1 tablespoon)

3 bay leaves

1 teaspoon oregano

1 can (1 pound) whole tomatoes

1 small jalapeño pepper, chopped (about 2 teaspoons)

2 teaspoons salt

1 pound dried red kidney beans, sorted to remove any stones and washed

1 bunch cilantro (coriander or Chinese parsley), stems and leaves chopped separately (¼ cup chopped stems, 2 teaspoons chopped leaves)

Heat the oil in a sturdy saucepan. When it is hot, add the pork in one layer and cook it over medium heat for about 30 minutes, turning it until it is brown on all sides.

Add 4 cups cold water and all the remaining ingredients except the chopped cilantro leaves. Bring to a boil, reduce the heat to low, cover, and simmer gently for 1¾ to 2 hours, until the meat is tender.

Divide among four individual plates, sprinkle with the chopped cilantro leaves, and serve with Yellow Rice with Orange Rind (see page 124).

Yield: 4 servings

Nutritional analysis per serving: calories 767; protein 46 gm.; carbohydrates 82 gm.; fat 29.7 gm.; saturated fat 9.6 gm.; cholesterol 85 mg.; sodium 1,400 mg.

Fillet of Pork Charcutière

For this classic pork recipe, pork fillets are trimmed of all fat, so they have no more cholesterol than chicken breasts and are also relatively low in calories. The acidic sauce served with the pork is particularly complementary. It consists of dried tomatoes and the liquid used to reconstitute them, onions, garlic, scallions, white wine, and *cornichons*, those tiny French-style gherkins preserved in vinegar. If these are not available at a specialty food store in your area, substitute standard commercial or homemade dill pickles to lend crunch and flavor to the dish.

1 ounce dried tomatoes

1 tablespoon unsalted butter

1 tablespoon virgin olive oil

2 pork fillets (about 10 ounces each), totally trimmed of fat and sinew and cut into 4 equal pieces (about 16 ounces total, trimmed)

½ cup red onion, cut into ¼-inch dice

1 teaspoon chopped garlic

⅓ cup minced scallions

¼ cup dry white wine

1 teaspoon Dijon-style mustard

¼ cup sliced cornichons (French-style gherkins)

¼ teaspoon salt

¼ teaspoon Tabasco sauce

Bring 1 cup water to a boil in a saucepan, add the dried tomatoes, and set aside for 30 to 45 minutes. Drain, reserving the soaking liquid (about ½ cup), and cut the tomatoes into ½-inch pieces. (You should have about 1 cup.)

Heat the butter and oil in a heavy skillet. When they are hot, add the meat and sauté it on one side for 4 to 5 minutes, then turn it over, cover the pan, reduce the heat, and cook the pork another 5 minutes.

Remove the meat to a plate, cover it, and set it aside to continue cooking in its own residual heat. Add the onion, garlic, and scallions to the skillet and sauté over medium to high heat for 1 minute. Stir in the wine and cook for 30 seconds. Add the reconstituted tomato pieces and their reserved soaking liquid. Bring to a boil and boil for 2 minutes to reduce the liquid. Then stir in the mustard, cornichons, salt, and Tabasco.

Arrange some of the sauce on top of and around each piece of meat and serve with Gnocchi *Maison* (see page 120).

Yield: 4 servings

Nutritional analysis per serving: calories 232; protein 26 gm.; carbohydrates 9 gm.; fat 9.5 gm.; saturated fat 3.2 gm.; cholesterol 81 mg.; sodium 448 mg.

Slow-Cooked Pork Roast

ften people don't realize that some cuts of pork—such as the loin and fillet I use here—are lean and very low in cholesterol and fat. This boneless sirloin roast from the end of the loin where it attaches to the fillet (or tenderloin) is so lean, in fact, that it would be dry if cooked in a conventional manner.

For the marinade

2 tablespoons soy sauce

1 tablespoon honey

½ teaspoon dry mustard

½ teaspoon ground ginger

1 teaspoon cumin powder

¼ teaspoon cayenne pepper

1 boneless pork sirloin roast, about 1½ pounds, trimmed of all surface fat

1 tablespoon canola oil

Preheat the oven to 275 degrees. Mix all the marinade ingredients together in a small bowl.

Place the roast in a roasting pan and rub it on all sides with the marinade. Roast it at 275 degrees for 2 hours, turning the meat in the juices every 45 minutes and adding a few tablespoons of water to the pan if a little additional moisture is needed. When the roast reaches an internal temperature of 155 degrees, add enough water to the pan to create about ½ cup of juice.

Cut the roast into ¼-inch slices and serve 3 slices per person with a generous spoonful of the juice.

Yield: 6 servings

Nutritional analysis per serving: calories 208; protein 24 gm.; carbohydrates 4 gm.; fat 10.1 gm.; saturated fat 2.8 gm.; cholesterol 72 mg.; sodium 400 mg.

Lamb Shanks and Beans Mulligan

This type of earthy stew is always welcome at my house when the temperature drops. Lamb shanks are by far the best cut for this; they remain moist while lending wonderful flavor to the stew. In addition, they are quite lean, which makes them less caloric than most other lamb cuts and milder, since it is the fat that gives lamb its distinctively "strong" taste. After the shanks are trimmed, any remaining visible fat in them melts as they are slowly browned. This fat can be discarded before the other ingredients are added to the casserole. ❦ Although the stew is great reheated, it may need to be thinned a little first. If necessary, add a few tablespoons of water to moisten the mixture before reheating it.

½ pound small white or Great Northern dried beans (about 1½ cups)

4 lamb shanks with bone (about 3 ½ pounds total)

1 carrot (4 ounces), peeled and cut into ½-inch pieces (¾ cup)

1 large onion (6 ounces), peeled and cut into 1-inch pieces (1¼ cups)

5 to 6 cloves garlic, peeled and coarsely chopped (1½ tablespoons)

3 bay leaves

1 teaspoon dried thyme leaves

1½ teaspoons salt

Tabasco sauce, to taste (optional)

Wash the beans in cool water and remove and discard any pebbles or damaged beans. Allow the beans to soak in the water while you brown the lamb shanks.

Remove most of the visible fat from the shanks. Place the shanks in one layer in a large, heavy casserole (preferably cast iron) and brown them, uncovered, over medium to high heat for 30 minutes, turning occasionally, until the meat is browned on all sides. Transfer the shanks to a plate and discard any fat rendered by the meat, leaving only a solidified glaze in the casserole.

Drain the beans and add them to the casserole with 3½ cups cold water and all the remaining ingredients except the optional Tabasco. Bring to a boil, uncovered, and then reduce the heat to low, cover, and boil gently for 2 hours.

At the end of the cooking period, the meat should be moist and tender and there should be just enough liquid remaining in the casserole to create a moist, thick stew. If there is substantially more liquid than this, boil the mixture, uncovered, for a few minutes to reduce it. Conversely, if there is too little liquid remaining, add a few tablespoons of water to extend it.

Serve one lamb shank per person, with a few spoonfuls of the stew. Pass the Tabasco sauce.

Yield: 4 servings

Nutritional analysis per serving: calories 570; protein 69 gm.; carbohydrates 44 gm.; fat 12.4 gm.; saturated fat 4.3 gm.; cholesterol 176 mg.; sodium 1,009 mg.

Couscous of Lamb

C ouscous is a national dish of the Maghreb, the fertile strip of land in North Africa comprising Morocco, Algeria, and Tunisia. There are variations between the couscous made in Algeria (which has tomato), Tunisia (which tends to be the hottest), and Morocco (which uses saffron). ❦ Couscous, the dish, takes its name from the wheat semolina of the same name that is one of its ingredients. A farinaceous grain, like rice and pasta, couscous is classically prepared in a *couscoussier* through a long, complicated steaming process. To simplify matters, I customarily use the instant couscous found in supermarkets, which is quite good. Couscous is usually served with meat, but it is sometimes combined with fish and vegetables, vegetables alone, or even fruit and sugar for a dessert not unlike rice pudding. ❦ When prepared as it is customarily with lamb or chicken, couscous is almost always served with a hot sauce, called *harissa* or *arissa*, which is a puree of hot peppers. I make my own *harissa* here, but it can be purchased in cans at some supermarkets and most specialty food stores. Some of this puree is mixed with the broth created by the stew and the remainder is served with the dish itself. ❦ The stew is quite liquid, but some of the liquid is used in the *harissa* and a lot is absorbed by the couscous.

For the harissa

2 ounces dried red chile pods (anchos) (6 to 8 peppers)

8 cloves garlic

2 tablespoons virgin olive oil

1 tablespoon tomato paste

1/4 teaspoon cayenne pepper

1/2 teaspoon salt

For the stew

1 1/2 pounds very lean lamb (preferably from the shank or shoulder), cut into 1 1/2-inch chunks

5 cloves garlic, peeled

1 piece fresh ginger about the same size as the combined garlic cloves, peeled

2 teaspoons cumin powder

2 teaspoons salt

2 tablespoons tomato paste

2 tablespoons homemade or canned harissa

1 large onion (8 ounces), peeled and sliced

1/2 pound kohlrabies or white turnips (about 2), peeled and cut into 1 1/2-inch chunks

1 small butternut squash (about 12 ounces), peeled, seeded, and cut into 1 1/2-inch chunks

1 small eggplant (about 8 ounces), trimmed and cut into 1 1/2-inch chunks

2 carrots (about 3 ounces), peeled and cut into 1 1/2-inch chunks

1 ripe tomato (about 8 ounces), cut in half, seeded, and cut into 1-inch dice

1 medium zucchini (about 6 ounces), washed and cut into 1 1/2-inch chunks

1 can (16 ounces) chick-peas (garbanzo beans)

For the couscous

¼ teaspoon freshly ground black pepper

¼ teaspoon salt

⅓ stick unsalted butter

2 cups instant couscous

4 ounces (about ¾ cup) dried figs, cut into ½-inch pieces

For the harissa: This recipe yields 1 cup, which is more than you need for the couscous, but *harissa* keeps under refrigeration for weeks and is excellent as a seasoning for stews, soups, or vegetable dishes.

Place the peppers in a bowl with 5 cups cold water. Set a plate on top to hold the peppers underwater and let them soak overnight.

Remove the peppers from the water and reserve ½ cup of the soaking water. Pull out and discard the pepper stems, and cut the peppers into 1-inch pieces. Place some of the pepper pieces in a mini-chop with some of the garlic, some of the oil, and a little of the pepper-soaking water, and process until pureed. Remove to a bowl. Process (in batches, if necessary) the remainder of the peppers with the remainder of the garlic, oil, and soaking liquid, and combine with the puree in the bowl. Add the tomato paste, cayenne, and salt to the puree, mix well, and place in a jar.

For the stew: If you like mild-flavored lamb, cover the lamb chunks with cold water, bring to a boil, drain in a colander, and rinse under cold water. Eliminate this step if you like stronger-flavored lamb. Place the lamb in a large dutch oven or pot and add 3 cups water.

Puree the garlic cloves and ginger together in a mini-chop or food processor (you will have about ¼ cup) and add the puree to the dutch oven with the cumin powder, salt, tomato paste, and *harissa*.

Bring the mixture to a boil and boil gently, covered, for 45 minutes. Add the onion, kohlrabies, butternut squash, eggplant, and carrots. Return to a boil and boil gently for 15 minutes. Then add the tomato, zucchini, and chick-peas with their liquid. Return to a boil and boil gently for 15 minutes longer. Set aside until serving time.

For the couscous: Bring 1¾ cups water to a boil in a small saucepan and add the pepper and salt. Meanwhile, melt the butter in a larger saucepan, add the couscous, and stir until the grains are coated with butter. Stir in the figs and then mix in the seasoned boiling water. Stir well, cover, and set aside for about 10 minutes.

For the harissa sauce: At serving time, place 1 cup of broth from the hot lamb stew into a serving bowl and add about 2 tablespoons (depending on the hotness you desire) of the homemade or canned *harissa*. Stir well and place the sauce on the table so guests can, at their discretion, add this to the stew.

To serve, fluff the couscous and mound it on individual plates. Make a well in the center of each mound and fill with a few pieces of meat, vegetables, and juice. Serve immediately.

Yield: 4 servings

Nutritional analysis per serving: calories 924; protein 57 gm.; carbohydrates 134 gm.; fat 18.4 gm.; saturated fat 7.6 gm.; cholesterol 129 mg.; sodium 1,817 mg.

Roasted Leg of Lamb

This traditional French bourgeois dish is great for entertaining, since even a small leg of lamb like this will easily serve eight people. Garlic slivers are customarily inserted into the flesh of the leg before it is cooked. In addition, I add a garnish of flavored bread crumbs, patting them onto the leg to form a beautiful coating. Carve the leg at the table in keeping with tradition. Leftovers can be served cold the following day with a salad.

1 small leg of spring lamb (5 pounds with shank and pelvis bone), trimmed of most visible fat, with pelvis bone removed (about 4 pounds, trimmed)

12 small slivers of garlic from one very large or 2 medium-size cloves of garlic

1½ tablespoons virgin olive oil

¼ teaspoon salt

¼ teaspoon freshly ground black pepper

2 cloves garlic, peeled

3 shallots, peeled

1½ cups (loose) flat parsley leaves

4 to 5 slices firm-textured white bread, processed to make crumbs in a food processor (2 cups)

Preheat the oven to 425 degrees. Make 12 small, randomly-placed incisions about ½ inch deep on both sides of the leg of lamb and insert a garlic sliver in each incision. Rub the leg with ½ tablespoon of the oil. Combine the salt and pepper and sprinkle on the lamb. Place the leg top side down in a roasting pan and roast it at 425 degrees for 15 minutes.

Meanwhile, place the peeled garlic, shallots, and parsley in the bowl of a food processor, and process until finely chopped. Place the bread crumbs in a bowl and gently stir in the processed mixture and the remaining table-spoon of oil, mixing just long enough to moisten the crumbs. (Don't overmix; the mixture should be loose, not gooey or lumpy.)

After 15 minutes, turn over the leg of lamb and pat the bread mixture on top. Reduce the oven temperature to 400 degrees and cook the lamb for another 30 minutes, until it reaches an internal temperature of about 130 degrees. Let it rest in a lukewarm place (on top of the stove or in a 180-degree oven) for 20 minutes before carving.

Yield: 8 servings

Nutritional analysis per serving: calories 298; protein 39 gm.; carbohydrates 8 gm.; fat 11.2 gm.; saturated fat 3.4 gm.; cholesterol 117 mg.; sodium 241 mg.

Veal Bitochki

This lean recipe for *bitochki*—the Russian name for ground meat patties—features ground veal, but ground turkey, chicken, or even beef could be used instead. To keep it moist and juicy, the meat is mixed with a combination of bread crumbs and milk before it is flavored with onion, garlic, parsley, salt, and pepper. ❦ The combination of horseradish and yogurt in the sauce gives it a distinctively Russian flavor that complements the veal nicely. To prevent the sauce from curdling, add the yogurt at the last minute and then don't heat the mixture above 160 degrees.

3 slices bread (about 2½ ounces)

½ cup milk

⅓ cup chopped onion

½ teaspoon chopped garlic

3 tablespoons chopped parsley

¼ teaspoon freshly ground black pepper

½ teaspoon salt

1 pound lean ground veal

For the horseradish-yogurt sauce

1 tablespoon virgin olive oil

2 tablespoons chopped onion

4 ounces mushrooms, washed and cut into julienne strips (1¾ cups)

¼ cup homemade chicken stock or canned chicken broth

1 tablespoon grated horseradish, either fresh or bottled

1 cup plain yogurt

¼ teaspoon salt

¼ teaspoon freshly ground black pepper

2 tablespoons coarsely chopped coriander (cilantro or Chinese parsley)

Process the bread into crumbs. (You should have 1½ cups.) Combine the crumbs and milk thoroughly in a bowl. Add the onion, garlic, parsley, pepper, and salt, and mix well. Mix in the ground veal. Divide the mixture into 4 patties, each about ¾ to 1 inch thick. Arrange the patties on a plate and place them in a steamer set over boiling water. Cook for 10 minutes, then remove them from the steamer and let them "rest" at room temperature while you prepare the sauce.

For the sauce: Heat the oil until it is hot but not smoking in a saucepan or skillet. Add the onion and sauté for 1 minute. Stir in the mushroom strips and cook for another 20 seconds. Add the stock, bring to a boil, and boil for about 2 minutes. Stir in the remainder of the ingredients and heat until warm, not boiling. (The sauce will break down if the mixture is brought to a boil.)

Serve the patties, one per person, coated with some of the sauce.

Yield: 4 servings

Nutritional analysis per serving: calories 317; protein 29 gm.; carbohydrates 19 gm.; fat 13.7 gm.; saturated fat 5.0 gm.; cholesterol 101 mg.; sodium 664 mg.

Fricassee of Veal

This recipe could serve as many as eight or as few as four, depending on the size of your guests' appetites and how extensive the menu is. For this type of recipe, it is best to make a large quantity; you can divide it afterward and freeze a portion for later. ❦ Be sure to use lean meat from the shoulder, chuck, or shank here. Meat from these parts of the animal will retain its moistness when stewed and will be much less expensive than meat from the back leg (top or bottom round), which is good for scaloppini but dry prepared in this manner. I finish this classic dish with cream, but that can be omitted and the dish can be served simply with the garnishes of onions and mushrooms.

1 tablespoon canola oil

1 tablespoon unsalted butter

2 pounds very lean veal from the shoulder, chuck, or shank, cut into 12 large cubes (2 inches each)

4 medium onions (12 ounces total), peeled and chopped (2½ cups)

2 tablespoons all-purpose flour

1 bouquet garni (see Bouquet Garni, page 161)

¾ teaspoon salt

5 cloves garlic, peeled, crushed, and coarsely chopped (1½ tablespoons)

For the garnishes

½ pound (12 to 15) pearl onions, peeled

½ pound mushrooms (domestic and/or wild), washed

⅓ cup heavy cream

Heat the oil and butter in a sturdy saucepan or dutch oven. When they are hot, add the meat and cook it over medium to low heat for 20 minutes, turning it often, until browned on all sides.

Add the chopped onion and cook for 5 minutes. Then add the flour and cook for 1 minute longer. Stir in 1½ cups water, the bouquet garni, the salt, and the garlic. Bring to a boil, cover, and boil gently for 1 hour. (The recipe can be prepared to this point up to one day ahead, cooled, and refrigerated.)

For the garnishes: Place the onions in a saucepan with ½ cup water. Bring to a boil and boil for 5 minutes. (Most of the water should have evaporated.) Add the onions with the mushrooms to the fricassee and boil gently 5 minutes. Sir in the cream and serve the fricassee with Wehani Brown Rice, page 125.

Yield: 6 servings

Nutritional analysis per serving: calories 306; protein 32 gm.; carbohydrates 12 gm.; fat 13.8 gm.; saturated fat 5.8 gm.; cholesterol 153 mg.; sodium 426 mg.

Grilled Veal Chops with Caper Sauce

T his is a good summer recipe. I use veal chops here, which are a good source of iron and zinc, but a breast of poultry or even a piece of fish would go well with the caper sauce. 🍒 If you are using veal, be sure you don't overcook it; although veal is not served rare as beef is, it should be slightly pink inside and juicy throughout. This is achieved by cooking the chops briefly on a very hot grill, to give them the distinctive taste and color of grilled meat, and then transferring them to a warm oven, where they continue to cook slowly in their own residual heat. The sauce is made separately and the chops coated with it before they are served.

4 veal rib chops, each about 1 inch thick (about 10 ounces each, with bones)

1 teaspoon canola oil

1/4 teaspoon salt

1/4 teaspoon freshly ground black pepper

For the caper and sage sauce

1/2 cup diced (1/4-inch dice) red onion

2 tablespoons capers

1 tablespoon minced fresh sage

2 teaspoons julienned lemon peel

1 tablespoon lemon juice

2 tablespoons virgin olive oil

2 tablespoons chopped flat parsley

1/4 teaspoon freshly ground black pepper

1/4 teaspoon salt

2 tablespoons homemade chicken stock or canned chicken broth

Heat a grill until it is very hot. Preheat the oven to 180 degrees. Rub the chops with the canola oil and sprinkle them with the 1/4 teaspoon each of salt and pepper. Cook the chops on the clean rack of the hot grill for about 2 1/2 minutes on each side. Transfer them to the 180-degree oven and let them rest for at least 10 minutes and no longer than 30 minutes before serving.

Meanwhile, mix all the sauce ingredients together in a bowl.

At serving time, place a chop on each of four plates and coat with the sauce.

Yield: 4 servings

Nutritional analysis per serving: calories 320; protein 35 gm.; carbohydrates 3 gm.; fat 18.0 gm.; saturated fat 3.8 gm.; cholesterol 155 mg.; sodium 519 mg.

Breast of Veal Cocotte

O f all meat juices, those rendered by veal have the most concentrated taste, especially when the veal is cooked slowly, as it is here, in a type of dutch oven or *cocotte*. I use veal breast, which is usually quite lean and relatively inexpensive. The amount of meat is small; at least two-thirds of the weight of a veal breast is bones and cartilage, both of which add flavor to the sauce. Carrots, onions, and garlic extend and enhance the dish.

1 veal breast, about 3½ pounds (4 to 5 meaty ribs)

1 tablespoon Herbes de Provence (see page 162)

½ teaspoon salt

1 tablespoon virgin olive oil

1 cup dry white wine

1 pound baby carrots (about 30), peeled

1 pound pearl onions (about 30), peeled

1 head garlic (15 to 20 cloves), peeled

Place the veal breast, *herbes de Provence*, salt, and olive oil in a large *cocotte* (a high-sided cooking pot or casserole with a lid) with ½ cup water. Bring to a boil over high heat, reduce the heat to medium, and boil, covered, for 15 minutes. At this point most of the liquid will have evaporated. Continue to cook, uncovered, over medium heat for about 25 minutes, turning the meat often to brown it well on all sides.

Add the wine, cover, reduce the heat to low, and simmer slowly for about 1¼ hours, until the meat is tender when pierced with a fork.

Mix in the carrots, onions, garlic, and ½ cup water. Cover and cook over low heat for 30 minutes longer.

Divide the meat, carrots, onions, and garlic among six individual plates and serve immediately.

Yield: 6 servings

Nutritional analysis per serving: calories 225; protein 18 gm.; carbohydrates 15 gm.; fat 10.5 gm.; saturated fat 3.7 gm.; cholesterol 69 mg.; sodium 290 mg.

Steak Maître d'Hôtel

Steak with Parsley Butter

W hen we think of steak, we usually think of an expensive beef tenderloin fillet or New York strip. This recipe, however, is prepared with any of a series of less expensive cuts, often called butcher steaks: One of these is from the shoulder blade; another—called an oyster steak—is from the hip; yet another, a hanging tenderloin—is from inside the rack. Other possibilities for this dish include a skirt steak, a flank steak, or—my choice—a triangle steak, the uppermost piece of a top sirloin, which comes from the hip. The beef should be totally defatted before it is cut into steaks approximately 6 ounces each. ❦ With the steaks, I serve a delicious parsley-flavored butter, known in France as *beurre maître d'hôtel*. It can be made ahead and will keep, refrigerated, for about a week. Leftover butter can be frozen for later use on grilled meat, poultry, or fish. It also makes a great final enrichment for soups.

For the parsley butter

2 tablespoons unsalted butter

2 tablespoons chopped parsley

1/8 teaspoon freshly ground black pepper

Small dash salt

1 tablespoon lemon juice

4 triangle beef steaks, from the hip (top sirloin), totally defatted (about 6 ounces each, 3/4 to 1 inch thick)

2 teaspoons canola oil

1/4 teaspoon salt

1/4 teaspoon black pepper

For the parsley butter: Place all the parsley butter ingredients in the bowl of a food processor and process until smooth.

At cooking time, rub both sides of the steaks with the oil, sprinkle them with the salt and pepper, and arrange them on the clean rack of a very hot grill. Cook for 1 1/2 to 2 minutes on each side for a medium rare steak.

Transfer the steaks to a platter and let them "rest" for about 5 minutes before serving. Spread about 1 1/2 teaspoons of the parsley butter on top of each steak and serve.

Yield: 4 servings

Nutritional analysis per serving: calories 294; protein 36 gm.; carbohydrates 0.5 gm.; fat 15.5 gm.; saturated fat 6.4 gm.; cholesterol 119 mg.; sodium 256 mg.

Daube of Beef in Red Wine

It is important in this recipe to use beef shoulder blade or shank. These are lean yet gelatinous cuts that will retain their moistness after cooking—a quality essential to the success of this dish. I cook the beef in a pressure cooker to save time. Being enclosed as it cooks also contributes to its moisture retention. ❧ An intensely flavored red wine sauce is the hallmark of this dish, and my recipe contains nearly a whole bottle of red wine, along with a little soy sauce, vinegar, garlic, onions, and carrots for flavor. Even though the dish is a bit complicated, it makes an outstanding winter main dish that is well worth the effort.

2 onions (about 8 ounces), peeled and quartered

2 carrots (about 6 ounces), washed and cut into 1-inch pieces

1 whole head garlic, separated into cloves (12 to 15), unpeeled

4 bay leaves

1 teaspoon dried thyme

1 teaspoon dried oregano

3 tablespoons red wine vinegar

4 tablespoons balsamic vinegar

2 tablespoons dark soy sauce

1 tablespoon black peppercorns, coarsely crushed

3 cups dry red wine (preferably a cabernet sauvignon variety or a deep, fruity red from the Rhône Valley)

1 piece of beef, about 3 pounds, from the shoulder blade (top blade) or a whole boned shank

1 tablespoon virgin olive oil

½ teaspoon salt

1 tablespoon potato starch dissolved in 2 tablespoons water

For the garnishes

About 18 small baby carrots (8 to 10 ounces total), peeled

About 18 small pearl onions (about 8 ounces total), peeled

About 18 small potatoes (about 1 pound total), peeled

About 18 medium mushrooms (about 12 ounces total)

1 tablespoon chopped parsley

Place the onions, carrots, garlic, bay leaves, thyme, oregano, vinegars, soy sauce, peppercorns, and red wine in a saucepan and bring the mixture to a boil over high heat. Meanwhile, place the meat in a heat-proof container. When the mixture in the saucepan comes to a boil, pour it over the meat and set it aside to cool. When it is cool, cover the container with plastic wrap, and refrigerate it for at least 6 hours and as long as 3 days.

When you are ready to cook, remove the beef, reserving the marinade, and pat the beef dry with paper towels. Heat the oil in a pressure cooker over medium to high heat until hot; then add the beef and sprinkle it with the salt. Cook, uncovered, over medium heat for about 15 minutes, turning occasionally, until the meat has browned on all sides. Add the marinade mixture and bring to a boil. Cover and bring the cooker to the appropriate pressure, following the manufacturer's guidelines. Then reduce the heat to very low and cook for 1 1/2 hours.

Depressurize the cooker according to the manufacturer's instructions and remove the meat. Transfer the cooking juices to a smaller saucepan and let them rest for 10 minutes to allow the fat to rise to the top. Place the meat back in the cooker.

Skim all visible fat from the surface of the juices and bring the remaining liquid to a boil. Boil gently for 5 minutes and then stir in the dissolved potato starch to thicken the juices. Using a strainer with a fine mesh, strain the resulting sauce and pour all but 1 cup of it over the meat.

For the garnishes: Place the carrots and onions in a saucepan with 1/2 cup water. Bring to a boil, cover, and boil over medium heat for 5 minutes. (Most of the liquid should be gone.) Set aside.

Place the potatoes in another saucepan and cover them with cold water. Bring to a boil and boil gently for 10 to 12 minutes, uncovered, until they are almost cooked but still firm. Drain and combine with the carrots and onions. Set aside until serving time.

Place the reserved cup of wine sauce in a large saucepan. Wash the mushrooms and add them to the sauce. Cover, bring to a boil, and boil gently for 5 minutes. Set aside until serving time.

At serving time, reheat the meat in the sauce over low heat until it is heated through. Add the carrots, onions, and potatoes to the mushrooms and heat until hot.

Arrange the meat on a large platter and cut it into 1-inch slices. Surround the meat with the vegetables and pour the sauce over and around them. Sprinkle with the parsley and serve.

Yield: 6 servings

Nutritional analysis per serving: calories 524; protein 49 gm.; carbohydrates 37 gm.; fat 19.7 gm.; saturated fat 6.7 gm.; cholesterol 148 mg.; sodium 838 mg.

ACCOMPANIMENTS

Ragout of Asparagus, page 108

Broccoli with Butter, page 109

Cucumber with Tarragon, page 110

Grilled Portobello Mushrooms, page 111

Stew of Peas and Ham, page 112

Darphin Potatoes, page 113

Potatoes Boulangère, page 114

Potato Sauté à Cru, page 115

Gratin of Tomato and Bread, page 116

Vegetable Burgers, page 117

Julienne of Zucchini, page 118

Oriental Savoy Salad, page 119

Gnocchi Maison, page 120

Coquillettes au Gruyère (Pasta Shells with Swiss Cheese), page 122

Bulgur Wheat Pilaf, page 123

Yellow Rice with Orange Rind, page 124

Wehani Brown Rice, page 125

Ragout of Asparagus

T his stew of asparagus can be ready in about 5 minutes and so should be prepared at the last moment. I find it worthwhile to peel the lower part of asparagus stalks. Removing the fibrous outer layer from the base of the tip to the cut end makes the entire spear edible; otherwise, only the tips are palatable. ❧ The spears can be peeled and cut in advance and refrigerated until cooking time. Most of the small amount of water used to cook the asparagus will evaporate, and the little bit remaining will mix and emulsify with the butter that is added at the end, creating a smooth, creamy, flavorful sauce. This dish makes an ideal first course.

16 asparagus spears (about 1 pound), peeled and cut into 1½-inch pieces (about 3 cups)

2 tablespoons unsalted butter

¼ teaspoon salt

Bring ½ cup water to a boil in a saucepan. Add the asparagus and bring the water back to a boil. Cover and boil for 2½ minutes over high heat. Add the butter and salt, bring back to a strong boil, and boil for about 1 minute longer. The cooking liquid will bind with the butter, creating a light, delicate sauce. Serve immediately.

Yield: 4 servings

Nutritional analysis per serving: calories 73; protein 3 gm.; carbohydrates 4 gm.; fat 6.0 gm.; saturated fat 3.6 gm.; cholesterol 16 mg.; sodium 138 mg.

Broccoli with Butter

P acked with beta-carotene and vitamin C, broccoli is low in calories and high in hunger-satisfying fiber. Choose bunches with heads that are very tight and deep green. I love this vegetable in everything from salads to soups, but this simple preparation is one of my favorites. Be sure, however, to peel the tough outer layer of the stems, so people eat the entire stalk, which I think is the best part of the broccoli. ❧ I cook the broccoli here in a minimum of water—most of it evaporates during the cooking time, leaving all the nutrients behind in the vegetable. I add a little butter for flavor at the last moment.

1 pound broccoli, separated into flowerets about 2 inches wide at the flower, with stems peeled (14 ounces peeled)

1½ tablespoons unsalted butter

¼ teaspoon salt

Place the broccoli in a large saucepan with 1 cup water. Bring to a boil and cook, covered, over medium heat for 5 minutes. (Most of the liquid will have evaporated.)

Add the butter and salt, mix gently, and serve immediately.

Yield: 4 servings

Nutritional analysis per serving: calories 66; protein 3 gm.; carbohydrates 5 gm.; fat 4.7 gm.; saturated fat 2.7 gm.; cholesterol 12 mg.; sodium 162 mg.

Cucumber with Tarragon

ven though cucumbers are usually eaten raw, cooked cucumbers make an absolutely delightful, light, and delicate garnish, particularly for fish. I use a "seedless" cucumber here and then cut it in such a way that most of the few seeds are trimmed away. The chopped tarragon is a welcome addition and gives the dish a special accent.

1 English-style "seedless" cucumber (about 1 pound)

1 tablespoon unsalted butter

¼ teaspoon salt

¼ teaspoon freshly ground black pepper

1 tablespoon chopped tarragon

Trim off and discard both ends of the cucumber and cut it crosswise into 1½ inch chunks. (You should have about 7 chunks.) Cut each chunk lengthwise into 6 wedges, and, using a small paring knife, round the sharp edges and shape the wedges into ovals, eliminating most of the seeds as you do so.

Bring 3 cups water to a boil in a saucepan. Add the cucumber ovals and bring the water back to a strong boil. Immediately drain the ovals in a sieve or colander and set aside.

At serving time, melt the butter in a large skillet. Add the cucumber ovals, salt, and pepper, and toss to mix. Cook 2 to 3 minutes, just until the ovals are hot throughout. Add the tarragon and toss it with the cucumber. Serve about 10 cucumber ovals per person.

Yield: 4 servings

Nutritional analysis per serving: calories 41; protein 1 gm.; carbohydrates 4 gm.; fat 3.0 gm.; saturated fat 1.8 gm.; cholesterol 8 mg.; sodium 138 mg.

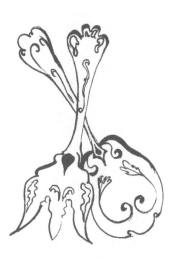

Grilled Portobello Mushrooms

These large, meaty, big-capped mushrooms are available now in most supermarkets around the country and are ideal for grilling. They make an attractive, flavorful, and unusual garnish for fish, poultry, or meat. I grill only the caps here, but the stems can be cooked alongside the caps on the grill or reserved and frozen for later use—preferably chopped, since they are tougher than the caps—in soups or stuffings.

4 large Portobello mushrooms (about 1 pound total), stems removed and reserved for soup or stuffing (12 ounces of caps)

1½ tablespoons virgin olive oil

¼ teaspoon salt

Preheat the oven to 180 degrees. Rub the top surface of the mushroom caps with the oil, which will be absorbed quickly, and sprinkle them with the salt.

Place the caps on a very hot grill and cook them, top side down, for 3 minutes. Then turn them over and cook them for 3 minutes on the other side.

If serving the mushrooms within 30 minutes, place them in a pan in a 180-degree oven until serving time. Otherwise, allow the mushrooms to cool and reheat them in a 400-degree oven or in a skillet on top of the stove just before serving.

Yield: 4 servings

Nutritional analysis per serving: calories 66; protein 2 gm.; carbohydrates 4 gm.; fat 5.4 gm.; saturated fat 0.7 gm.; cholesterol 0 mg.; sodium 138 mg.

Stew of Peas and Ham

This is the type of cooking my mother used to do when I was a child. She would add a little flour to sautéed onions to make a roux, as I do here, and then use this as a base for a fricassee or stew. ❧ When fresh peas are in season, I use them in this recipe, but frozen baby peas can be substituted and the cooking time reduced from about 8 to 2 or 3 minutes. Fresh peas yield the bonus of their pods, which I use for Pea Pod Soup, page 22. ❧ While this stew is a fine garnish for meat, poultry, or fish, it also makes a great first course for dinner or main course for a light lunch.

1½ teaspoons unsalted butter

1½ teaspoons corn or canola oil

1 onion (4 ounces), chopped (¾ cup)

2 scallions, minced (⅓ cup)

1½ teaspoons flour

3 carrots (6 ounces), peeled and cut into ½-inch pieces

½ teaspoon salt

¼ teaspoon freshly ground black pepper

¼ teaspoon Herbes de Provence (see page 162)

1 pound fresh peas, shelled (6 ounces, 1¼ cups), with pods reserved for Pea Pod Soup, page 22

⅔ cup diced (½-inch dice) ham (2½ ounces)

Heat the butter and oil in a saucepan. When they are hot, add the onion and scallions, and sauté over medium to high heat for 2 minutes. Add the flour and mix well. Stir in 1½ cups water and add the carrots, salt, pepper, and *herbes de Provence*. Bring the mixture to a boil, cover, and boil for 2 minutes.

Add the peas to the saucepan and bring the mixture to a boil again. Cover, reduce the heat to low, and boil gently for about 8 minutes, or until the peas are as tender as you like. Add the ham, mix well, and bring to a boil. (You should have 2½ cups.) Serve.

Yield: 4 servings

Nutritional analysis per serving: calories 119; protein 7 gm.; carbohydrates 14 gm.; fat 4.3 gm.; saturated fat 1.4 gm.; cholesterol 12 mg.; sodium 544 mg.

Darphin Potatoes

For this recipe, raw potatoes are shredded, pressed into a nonstick pan, and cooked, creating a kind of compact cake. The result is similar to what the Swiss call *rösti* potatoes and the French in the Lyon area where I come from call *paillasson*, which, literally translated, means "doormat"—an object the tightly compressed sautéed potato strands resemble. This dish is excellent with any kind of roast or on its own with a salad.

1½ pounds baking potatoes (about 3)

1 tablespoon unsalted butter

1 tablespoon corn oil

4 scallions, chopped (½ cup)

½ teaspoon salt

¼ teaspoon freshly ground black pepper

When ready to cook the potatoes, peel them and rinse them under cold tap water. Using the side of a cheese grater with the larger holes, shred the potatoes. (You should have about 4 cups.)

Heat the butter and oil in a nonstick skillet until hot. Add the potatoes, scallions, salt, and pepper, and sauté, stirring occasionally, for about 2 minutes, until the potatoes are mixed well with the seasonings. Press on the mixture with a spoon to compact it, cover, reduce the heat, and cook gently for about 12 minutes on one side. Flip the potato mixture over and cook it for 10 minutes on the other side. Invert it onto a serving plate, cut into wedges, and serve as soon as possible.

Yield: 4 servings

Nutritional analysis per serving: calories 161; protein 3 gm.; carbohydrates 24 gm.; fat 6.4 gm.; saturated fat 2.2 gm.; cholesterol 8 mg.; sodium 284 mg.

Potatoes Boulangère

P*ommes de terre à la boulangère* is the classic garnish for Roasted Leg of Lamb (see page 98) in France and, translated literally, means "baker's wife potatoes." My version of this dish is made with a lean, unsalted chicken stock and flavored with lots of onion. Wine is added for a dash of acidity. It is important to cook the potatoes long enough; while they should be soft and moist, most of the liquid surrounding them should be gone—evaporated or absorbed by the potatoes. ❧ The potatoes can be peeled ahead and set aside in water to cover, but don't slice them until just before the dish is assembled. Soaking potatoes in water extracts starch from them and the smaller the potato pieces, the greater the amount of starch drawn out. Since some starch is needed as a thickening agent here, it is best not to slice the potatoes before soaking them.

---

2 pounds boiling potatoes, peeled and placed in water to cover

1 tablespoon peanut oil

4 onions (about 14 ounces total), peeled and cut into thin slices (4 cups)

6 cloves garlic, peeled and cut into thin slices (3 tablespoons)

3 cups unsalted chicken stock

1 teaspoon salt

½ teaspoon freshly ground black pepper

½ cup dry white wine

A seasoning package consisting of 3 bay leaves and 1 teaspoon thyme leaves, tied up in cheesecloth (see Bouquet Garni, page 161)

Preheat the oven to 375 degrees. Cut the potatoes into ⅛-inch-thick slices.

Heat the oil in a saucepan. When it is hot, add the onions and sauté them for 3 to 4 minutes. Add the remainder of the ingredients except the seasoning package and transfer the mixture to an 8-cup gratin dish. Place the seasoning package in the center, pressing it lightly into the potatoes.

Bake the gratin at 375 degrees for 50 minutes to 1 hour, until most of the moisture is absorbed and the potatoes are tender when pierced with a fork. Remove and discard the seasoning package and serve the gratin immediately.

Yield: 8 servings

Nutritional analysis per serving: calories 141; protein 4 gm.; carbohydrates 25 gm.; fat 2.5 gm.; saturated fat 0.5 gm.; cholesterol 0 mg.; sodium 304 mg.

Potato Sauté à Cru

P otatoes that are sautéed raw have a totally different taste from hash browns, which are made from cooked potatoes. ❧ For this dish, the potatoes can be peeled and even sliced ahead, as long as they are kept in water to cover and then are carefully drained and patted dry just before sautéing. ❧ Cook the potatoes in oil, as indicated in the recipe. If you want the flavor of butter, add a little at the end of the cooking period for maximum taste enhancement. Oil can withstand higher temperatures than butter without burning, and, to brown these potatoes properly, you must cook them at a fairly high temperature. ❧ This dish is best served immediately after cooking—20 minutes is the maximum waiting time. If it is prepared ahead and reheated, the taste will be disappointingly different.

4 baking potatoes (1¾ to 2 pounds)

3 tablespoons canola oil

¼ teaspoon salt

Peel the potatoes and cut them crosswise into ¼-inch slices. Rinse them and set them aside in a bowl of cool water to cover. (This can be done a couple of hours ahead.)

About 20 minutes before serving, drain the potato slices and pat them dry with paper towels.

Heat the oil in one very large or two smaller skillets (preferably nonstick). When it is hot, add the potatoes and cook them over medium to high heat, half covered (to prevent splattering), for about 15 minutes, tossing them every 2 minutes or so to prevent them from burning and enable them to brown on all sides. (Some of the slices will be browner than others, but this gives contrast of texture, color, and taste to the dish.) When the potatoes are tender, toss them with the salt. Serve immediately.

Yield: 4 servings

Nutritional analysis per serving: calories 217; protein 3 gm.; carbohydrates 29 gm.; fat 10.4 gm.; saturated fat 0.8 gm.; cholesterol 0 mg.; sodium 145 mg.

Gratin of Tomato and Bread

his is a terrific summer dish; cherry tomatoes are inexpensive then and at their peak. For variety, I sometimes substitute yellow cherry tomatoes for the red or use small pear-shaped tomatoes. The combination of flavors—tomatoes, bread, garlic, olive oil, parsley, and parmesan cheese—makes this everybody's favorite.

1¼ pounds cherry tomatoes (about 3½ cups)

3 ounces day-old bread (preferably from a French baguette), cut into 1-inch cubes (about 3½ cups)

6 cloves garlic, peeled and sliced (2 tablespoons)

½ cup coarsely chopped parsley

½ teaspoon freshly ground black pepper

2 tablespoons virgin olive oil

½ teaspoon salt

¼ cup grated parmesan cheese

Preheat the oven to 375 degrees. Wash the tomatoes and remove and discard any stems. Place the tomatoes in a bowl and mix in the remainder of the ingredients. Transfer the mixture to a 6-cup gratin dish. Bake at 375 degrees for 40 minutes. Serve immediately.

Yield: 4 servings

Nutritional analysis per serving: calories 185; protein 6 gm.; carbohydrates 21 gm.; fat 9.4 gm.; saturated fat 2.1 gm.; cholesterol 5 mg.; sodium 506 mg.

Vegetable Burgers

For this interesting recipe, several vegetables are first cooked together. I use spinach, corn, peas, and red pepper, but other vegetables could be substituted. The vegetable cooking juices—in combination with some chicken stock—are used as a base for cooking the grits. While I use white grits here, semolina or farina could also be used to create the thick mass needed to hold the vegetables together. ❧ The burgers can be assembled in advance but should not be sautéed until the last moment. Be sure to sauté them in a nonstick pan and turn them carefully with a large hamburger spatula. Although they are moist and delicious, they are delicate and have a tendency to break apart.

3 cups (loosely packed) trimmed and washed spinach

1 ear sweet corn, husked, with kernels removed ($\frac{1}{2}$ cup)

$\frac{1}{2}$ cup fresh peas or frozen baby peas

$\frac{1}{3}$ cup peeled (with a vegetable peeler), diced ($\frac{1}{4}$-inch dice) red bell pepper

1$\frac{1}{4}$ cups chicken stock

$\frac{1}{2}$ teaspoon salt

$\frac{1}{4}$ teaspoon freshly ground black pepper

$\frac{1}{2}$ cup white grits

1$\frac{1}{2}$ tablespoons canola oil

$\frac{1}{2}$ teaspoon unsalted butter

Bring 1 cup water to a boil in a saucepan. Add the spinach, corn kernels, peas, and red pepper, and bring the water back to a boil. Immediately drain the vegetables in a colander set over a pan, pressing lightly on the vegetables to extrude most of the water. You should have about 1 cup of cooking liquid.

Place the cooking liquid in a saucepan with the chicken stock, salt, and pepper, and bring to a boil. Add the grits and mix well. Cook, covered, over low heat, stirring occasionally so the grits don't stick to the bottom of the pan, for 20 to 25 minutes. The mixture will be quite thick.

Transfer the grits to a dish, spreading them out so they cool more quickly. When they are lukewarm, add the vegetables and mix well. Cool completely and then form the mixture into four patties.

At serving time, heat the oil and butter in a nonstick pan. When they are hot, add the patties and cook, covered (to prevent splattering), for about 8 minutes on the first side. Turn carefully (the patties tend to break apart) and cook for another 8 minutes on the second side. Serve.

Yield: 4 servings

Nutritional analysis per serving: calories 177; protein 6 gm.; carbohydrates 25 gm.; fat 6.7 gm.; saturated fat 0.9 gm.; cholesterol 1 mg.; sodium 333 mg.

Julienne of Zucchini

The zucchini are cut in an interesting way here: Long, thin strips are sliced from the firm, fleshy sides of the vegetable and the cottony, seedy centers are discarded. When sliced this way, into what we call julienne strips, zucchini has a special "bite" and crunchiness, and it makes an attractive presentation. You can also make a "nest" of these strips and serve them topped with a grilled lamb chop, scallops, shrimp, or fish. Zucchini are low in calories and high in vitamins A and C and potassium.

4 or 5 small, firm zucchini (about 1½ pounds total)

1 tablespoon unsalted butter

2 tablespoons virgin olive oil

4 tablespoons chopped shallots

¼ teaspoon salt

¼ teaspoon freshly ground black pepper

Wash the zucchini and trim off and discard both ends. Using a mandoline or a sharp knife, cut each zucchini lengthwise into long julienne strips ⅛ inch thick, stopping when you reach the cottony center of the zucchini. Rotate the zucchini and continue cutting until all the firm flesh has been removed. Discard the centers and set aside the julienne strips. (You should have about 6 cups.)

Heat the butter and oil in a large skillet. When they are hot, add the shallots and sauté for 15 seconds over medium to high heat. Add the zucchini, salt, and pepper, and sauté over high heat for 4 minutes.

Serve immediately.

Yield: 4 servings

Nutritional analysis per serving: calories 116; protein 2 gm.; carbohydrates 7 gm.; fat 9.9 gm.; saturated fat 2.7 gm.; cholesterol 8 mg.; sodium 142 mg.

Oriental Savoy Salad

S avoy cabbage is quite attractive, with its pale and darker green colors, and its wrinkled leaves tend to hold a dressing well. I macerate the leaves here in an interesting mixture containing oyster sauce and garlic that goes particularly well with the cabbage. This salad is great as a garnish for roasted or grilled poultry, meat, or fish, and it also makes a good first course.

For the Oriental dressing

2 tablespoons rice wine vinegar

1½ tablespoons soy sauce

1 tablespoon oyster sauce

¼ teaspoon Tabasco sauce

1 teaspoon sugar

2 cloves garlic, peeled, crushed, and finely chopped (2 teaspoons)

½ pound tender savoy cabbage leaves, with tough lower part of central ribs removed and discarded, leaves shredded fine (about 6 cups, lightly packed)

½ cup julienned carrot strips

Combine the dressing ingredients in a plastic bag large enough to hold the cabbage. Add the cabbage, toss it with the dressing, and allow the mixture to macerate for at least 2 hours.

Transfer the salad and dressing to a serving bowl, sprinkle with the carrot, and serve.

Yield: 4 servings

Nutritional analysis per serving: calories 34; protein 2 gm.; carbohydrates 7 gm.; fat 0.1 gm.; saturated fat 0 gm.; cholesterol 0 mg.; sodium 585 mg.

Gnocchi Maison

Thmere are different types of gnocchi: Roman-style gnocchi are made with semolina that is first cooked into a mush and then cooled, molded, and cut into shapes; potato gnocchi, another type, use potatoes as the main ingredient; Parisian gnocchi are made with a *pâte à choux* (cream puff dough) mixture. ❦ For this recipe, I use elements of both the potato and the Parisian gnocchi. The mixture can be prepared and even poached ahead, either by dropping spoonfuls of it into boiling water or piping it, as I do here, from a pastry bag held directly over the pot. As the mixture emerges from the bag, I cut it at the tip into 1/2-inch lengths and let them drop into the pot. This technique is faster and produces gnocchi of a more uniform size and shape than the spoon method. ❦ Gnocchi make an excellent garnish for poultry, fish, or meat.

1 medium potato (about 5 ounces)

2 tablespoons virgin olive oil

1/4 teaspoon salt

1/8 teaspoon freshly ground black pepper

1/2 cup all-purpose flour

2 tablespoons parmesan cheese

2 eggs

2 tablespoons chopped parsley

Place the potato in a small saucepan and cover it with water. Bring to a boil, cover, reduce the heat to low, and boil gently for about 40 minutes, until tender. Drain and let cool. When the potato is cool enough to handle, peel it. Set aside.

Place 1/2 cup water, 1 tablespoon of the oil, the salt, and the pepper in a saucepan and bring to a boil. Remove from the heat and add the flour all at once. Mix well with a wooden spoon until the mixture forms a ball, and then place the pan back over the heat for 15 or 20 seconds to dry out the dough a little.

Preheat the oven to 400 degrees. Bring 5 cups water to a boil in a saucepan. Meanwhile, transfer the ball of dough to the bowl of a food processor and add the potato in pieces. Process for about 10 seconds. Add 1 tablespoon of the cheese and 1 of the eggs, and process for 5 seconds. Add the other egg and process until smooth. Place the mixture in a pastry bag fitted with a 3/4-inch plain round tip.

Pipe the mixture from the pastry bag into the boiling water, cutting it with a knife into 1/2-inch pieces as it emerges from the tip and letting the pieces drop into the water. (You should have 35 to 40 pieces.) Bring the water back to a light boil, reduce the heat, and boil very gently, uncovered, for 5 minutes.

With a slotted spoon, transfer the gnocchi to a bowl of ice water. When they are cold, drain them and place them in a 3- to 4-cup gratin dish. Add the remaining tablespoon each of oil and cheese along with the parsley, and mix well.

At serving time, heat the gnocchi in the oven at 400 degrees for 12 to 15 minutes and serve immediately.

Yield: 4 servings

Nutritional analysis per serving: calories 187; protein 6 gm.; carbohydrates 17 gm.; fat 10.2 gm.; saturated fat 2.2 gm.; cholesterol 108 mg.; sodium 216 mg.

Coquillettes au Gruyère

Pasta Shells with Swiss Cheese

f you are serving this dish with *Poulet Rôti* (see page 86), replace the olive oil with a little of the fat that emerges from the chicken and the deglazed drippings from the skillet in which the chicken was roasted. This unites the pasta with the taste of the chicken, making them wonderfully compatible.

10 ounces medium-size pasta shells, preferably imported

3 tablespoons virgin olive oil

½ teaspoon salt

¼ teaspoon freshly ground black pepper

1 tablespoon chives

1 cup (loosely packed) freshly grated swiss cheese (3 ounces), preferably Gruyère

Bring 2 quarts water to a boil in a saucepan. Add the pasta and cook until tender (about 15 minutes). Remove ½ cup of the pasta-cooking liquid and put it in a stainless steel bowl large enough to hold the shells. Then drain the pasta in a colander.

To the cooking liquid in the bowl add the olive oil, salt, and pepper. Mix well. Add the pasta and chives, toss to mix, and stir in the cheese.

Spoon the pasta onto four plates and serve immediately.

Yield: 4 servings

Nutritional analysis per serving: calories 441; protein 15 gm.; carbohydrates 53 gm.; fat 18.1 gm.; saturated fat 5.5 gm.; cholesterol 23 mg.; sodium 350 mg.

Bulgur Wheat Pilaf

Bulgur is a steamed and dried cracked wheat that is reconstituted for use by soaking it in hot water for about 1 hour or cold water for at least 2 hours, or by boiling it in water for about 30 minutes. The quality of bulgur varies; I prefer to buy mine in health food stores, because I find their version is generally composed of bigger pieces rather than just flakes and is much less expensive than the packaged bulgur available in supermarkets. This grain has a chewy, nutty texture that makes it particularly good with stews or roasted meats or poultry. I especially like it with Chicken Supreme Kiev-Style, page 84.

½ cup cracked bulgur wheat

1 tablespoon peanut oil

1 red onion (5 ounces), peeled and chopped (1¼ cups)

2 cloves garlic, peeled, crushed, and chopped (1 teaspoon)

¼ teaspoon salt

⅛ teaspoon freshly ground black pepper

½ cup frozen petite peas

1½ teaspoons unsalted butter

Place the bulgur in a heat-proof bowl and pour 1½ cups boiling water over it. Let stand for 45 minutes to 1 hour, until most of the water is absorbed by the wheat. Drain in a sieve.

Heat the peanut oil in a saucepan. When the oil is hot, sauté the onion in it for about 3 minutes. Add the garlic, salt, and pepper, and sauté for 10 seconds.

Stir the drained bulgur into the mixture in the saucepan. Cook for 4 to 5 minutes. Excess moisture will cook away initially and then the wheat will begin to brown and become fluffy. Add the frozen peas, mix well, and cook for about 1 minute longer. Stir in the butter.

Serve immediately with Chicken Supreme Kiev-Style, page 84.

Yield: 4 servings

Nutritional analysis per serving: calories 132; protein 4 gm.; carbohydrates 19 gm.; fat 5.2 gm.; saturated fat 1.5 gm.; cholesterol 4 mg.; sodium 174 mg.

Yellow Rice with Orange Rind

A merican Indians painted their faces with the dye from achiote seeds. Virtually tasteless, they lend bright color to the rice. They soften somewhat after cooking and are edible, but you can sauté them in the oil and butter until they have released their color and then remove and discard them before adding the onions and pepper flakes to the pan. For a more conventional white rice, omit the achiote seeds and orange rind.

1 tablespoon canola oil

1½ teaspoons unsalted butter

1 cup chopped onions

1 teaspoon achiote (annatto) seeds

¼ teaspoon crushed red pepper flakes

1 cup long-grain white rice

½ teaspoon salt

1½ teaspoons grated orange rind

Heat the oil and butter in a saucepan. When they are hot, add the onions, achiote seeds, and red pepper flakes. Cook over medium heat for 3 to 4 minutes.

Mix in the rice. Add 2 cups water, the salt, and the orange rind. Bring to a boil, cover, reduce the heat to low, and cook gently for 20 minutes. Serve with Puerto Rican Pork and Beans, page 92.

Yield: 4 servings

Nutritional analysis per serving: calories 228; protein 4 gm.; carbohydrates 41 gm.; fat 5.2 gm.; saturated fat 1.2 gm.; cholesterol 4 mg.; sodium 277 mg.

Wehani Brown Rice

I was first introduced to wehani rice a few years ago, and it has since become one of my favorites. The extra-long, reddish brown kernels require a long time to cook, but they then have a nutty, chewy texture that I love. Even though wehani rice is not available everywhere in the country, it is carried or can be ordered by many health food stores. It is well worth the search!

2 tablespoons virgin olive oil

1 medium onion (5 ounces), peeled and chopped (1 cup)

⅓ cup pumpkin seeds

1 cup (6 ounces) wehani brown rice

¾ teaspoon salt

Heat the olive oil in a saucepan until it is hot but not smoking. Add the onion and sauté for 2 minutes. Then add the pumpkin seeds and cook for 1 minute. Mix in the rice thoroughly and add the salt and 2½ cups warm water. Bring to a boil, stirring occasionally. Cover, reduce the heat to low, and boil gently for 1 hour, or until the water has been absorbed by the rice and it is tender. Serve immediately.

Yield: 4 servings

Nutritional analysis per serving: calories 253; protein 5 gm.; carbohydrates 38 gm.; fat 9.1 gm.; saturated fat 1.3 gm.; cholesterol 0 mg.; sodium 417 mg.

DESSERTS

Country Apple Tart, page 128

Cheese, Apple, and Nut Mélange, page 130

Pain au Chocolat and Noisettes (Bread with Chocolate and Hazelnuts), page 131

Banana Tartlets, page 132

Crunchy Horns with Fruit, page 134

Prickly Meringues with Fruit Sauce, page 136

Guava Paste Toast with Mint, page 137

Apricot and Fig Soufflé, page 138

Café au Lait Granité, page 139

Crêpes à la Confiture, page 140

Jam Omelet Soufflé, page 141

Frozen Black Velvet, page 142

Custard with Blueberry Sauce, page 143

Blueberry Crumble, page 144

Russian Cranberry Kissel, page 145

Grapefruit and Kiwi Ambrosia, page 146

Prunes and Grapefruit in Red Wine Sauce, page 147

Grapes in Red Wine Sauce, page 148

Pears au Gratin, page 149

Pears in Espresso, page 150

Pineapple Delice, page 151

Potted Plums with Phyllo Dough, page 152

Strawberries in the Sun, page 153

Glazed Strawberries, page 154

Country Apple Tart

I make this tart—possibly the most "French" of all desserts—often at home and especially like it for buffet-style entertaining. Guests pick up pieces as they would slices of pizza and eat them lukewarm or at room temperature. It is a difficult dessert to make for four, so I have enough here for eight. Any leftovers will disappear quickly enough! ❦ The dough, made with only a cup of flour, should be rolled very thin. The tart can be made in a conventional pie mold or tart ring, but I do it free-form instead, so that no trimming is necessary and all the dough is used. The finished tart has a wonderfully rustic, "country" look. ❦ It is important that you use only the amount of apples called for in the recipe. People tend to use more, thinking it will make the tart even better, but a thin layer of apples is more effective. Be sure to cook the tart for a long time—at least an hour; the pastry should be dark brown and crusty and the apples tender.

For the tart dough

1 cup all-purpose flour (about 5 ounces)

1 tablespoon sugar

2½ ounces (⅔ stick) cold unsalted butter, cut into ½-inch pieces

2½ tablespoons ice water

4 golden delicious apples (1¾ pounds total)

1 tablespoon honey

2 tablespoons sugar

½ teaspoon cinnamon

1 tablespoon unsalted butter

For the tart dough: Place the flour, sugar, and butter in the bowl of a food processor and process for about 5 seconds. Add the water and process for about 10 seconds, until the dough just begins to come together. Refrigerate the dough while you prepare the apples.

Preheat the oven to 400 degrees. Peel, halve, and core the apples. Then arrange them, cut side down, on a cutting board and cut them crosswise into ¼-inch slices. Set aside the larger center slices, and chop the end slices and any broken slices coarsely. (About half the slices should be sliced, half chopped.)

On a lightly floured, flat work surface, roll the dough to create a 12-by-14-inch rectangle. Transfer the dough rectangle to a cookie sheet.

Arrange the chopped apples on the dough, spreading them out to within 1 inch of the edge. Sprinkle the honey over the chopped apples. Arrange the apple slices in one slightly overlapping layer on top of the chopped apples, positioning them to imitate the petals of a flower.

In a small bowl, mix together the sugar and cinnamon. Sprinkle this mixture on top of the sliced apples and dot them with the butter.

Fold the edge of the pastry over the apples to create a 1-inch border. Bake the tart at 400 degrees for 60 minutes, until the pastry is brown and crisp and the apples tender. Cut the tart into eight pieces and serve it lukewarm or at room temperature.

Yield: 8 servings

Nutritional analysis per serving: calories 215; protein 2 gm.; carbohydrates 33 gm.; fat 9.0 gm.; saturated fat 5.4 gm.; cholesterol 23 mg.; sodium 2 mg.

Cheese, Apple, and Nut Mélange

This combination of cheese, nuts, and apples that have been rolled in lemon juice and sprinkled with black pepper is delicious. ❧ To coarsely crush whole peppercorns (creating what the French call a *mignonnette*), spread the peppercorns on a clean, flat surface, and press on them with the base of a saucepan until they crack open. Pepper crushed this way has a better flavor and is much less hot than pepper ground conventionally in a pepper mill. If you must use a mill, however, set it to grind the pepper as coarsely as possible. ❧ I serve the mélange as a dessert, but it also makes an ideal brunch or light lunch main dish.

2 large apples (russet, golden delicious, or Rome Beauty)

2 tablespoons lemon juice

½ teaspoon black peppercorns, coarsely crushed (mignonnette)

⅔ cup pecans (about 25 halves)

5 ounces blue cheese (Gorgonzola, Stilton, or Roquefort), cut into 4 pieces

4 sprigs basil or arugula (about 5 ounces)

French bread

Preheat the oven to 375 degrees. Cut the unpeeled apples into quarters, remove and discard the cores, and roll the quarters in the lemon juice. Sprinkle the apples with the pepper. Spread the pecans on a cookie sheet and bake at 375 degrees for 8 minutes.

To serve, arrange 2 pieces of apple, 1 piece of cheese, and a few pecans on each of four plates. Arrange a few leaves from the basil or arugula sprigs around the apples. Serve with crusty French bread.

Yield: 4 servings

Nutritional analysis per serving: calories 303; protein 10 gm.; carbohydrates 18 gm.; fat 22.8 gm.; saturated fat 7.7 gm.; cholesterol 27 mg.; sodium 511 mg.

Pain au Chocolat and Noisettes

Bread with Chocolate and Hazelnuts

Eating a piece of crusty *ficelle* (French "string" bread) and a chunk of bittersweet chocolate together takes me back to my youth. As children, my brother and I typically enjoyed this combination for our after-school snack. Even though I occasionally sample the updated, more refined version of *pain au chocolat*—rolled *croissant* dough with a piece of chocolate inside—my preference is still for the original version of this treat that I loved as a child. I serve it here as a dessert with some toasted hazelnuts and grapes. The combined flavors of these disparate ingredients are wonderful! ❦ Toasting the hazelnuts in their shells has advantages. Protected by the shells, the nuts keep—don't get rancid—for weeks longer than when shelled before roasting; they retain their rich, roasted taste, even if not cracked open and eaten until weeks later.

4 dozen hazelnuts in their shells (about 7 ounces)

1 large bunch (16 ounces) seedless green grapes

1 ficelle bread loaf (see page 163)

1 piece (about 6 ounces) bittersweet chocolate

Preheat the oven to 400 degrees. Spread the unshelled hazelnuts on a cookie sheet and bake them at 400 degrees for about 15 minutes to toast them lightly inside. Cool.

Wash the grapes (do not pull them from the stems) and separate them into four small bunches.

Arrange a bunch of grapes on each of four plates. Crack the shells of the hazelnuts and divide them among the plates along with a piece of *ficelle.* Break the chocolate into four pieces and place a piece on each plate. Eat the crusty bread, chocolate, hazelnuts, and grapes together.

Yield: 4 servings

Nutritional analysis per serving: calories 521; protein 10 gm.; carbohydrates 63 gm.; fat 32.3 gm.; saturated fat 10.8 gm.; cholesterol 0 mg.; sodium 108 mg.

Banana Tartlets

This tartlet dough recipe contains only half a cup of flour and four tablespoons of butter, which is remarkably little considering it serves four. Also, since a quarter to a third of the dough will be trimmed away when it is pressed into shells for baking, an even smaller amount of these ingredients will actually be consumed in this dessert. The pastry cream is similarly deceptive: Although it contains a cup of milk, it has only one egg yolk and one tablespoon of cornstarch, so it is much less caloric than a conventional pastry cream. ❦ The tartlet shells can be made as much as a day ahead, but should not be filled with the pastry cream and fruit until just before serving. You can eliminate the pastry cream altogether, if you prefer, and fill the shells with sliced bananas or another fresh fruit.

For the tartlet shells

½ cup all-purpose flour

3 tablespoons unsalted butter

1½ teaspoons canola oil

1½ teaspoons sugar

1 tablespoon milk

For the pastry cream

1 cup milk

1 egg yolk

2 tablespoons sugar

1 teaspoon pure vanilla extract

1 tablespoon cornstarch

1 large ripe banana (10 ounces)

½ cup apricot preserves

1 tablespoon kirsch

4 dates, pitted and thinly sliced

For the tartlet shells: Preheat the oven to 400 degrees. Place the flour, butter, oil, and sugar in the bowl of a food processor and process for 10 seconds. Add the milk and process just until the mixture forms a ball.

Transfer the ball of dough to a board and roll it between two sheets of plastic wrap to form an 8-inch square approximately ⅛ inch thick. Arrange four tartlet shells (3 inches in diameter by ½ inch deep) side by side in two rows. Remove the sheet of plastic wrap from the top of the dough and, supporting the dough with the plastic wrap underneath, invert it over the tartlet shells.

Peel off the remaining sheet of plastic wrap and use it to press the dough lightly into the shells. Then run your rolling pin directly over the tops of the shells to trim away excess dough. Remove and reserve the dough trimmings. (They will amount to about a quarter of the dough.)

To make the dough adhere well to the bottoms and sides of the shells, dust your hands lightly with flour and press the dough firmly into each shell. To prevent the dough from collapsing while cooking, line each of the shells with wax paper or aluminum foil and fill them with rice or lead pellets. Or, if you have enough extra shells, place an empty one on each of the pastry-lined shells and press down on it lightly to hold the dough in position during cooking. Arrange the shells on a cookie sheet. Wrap the reserved dough trimmings well and refrigerate or freeze them for later use or lay them flat on a cookie sheet and bake them with the tartlets to eat as a snack.

Bake the pastry at 400 degrees for 10 minutes. Remove the empty shells or weight-filled wax paper or foil and bake the pastry for 5 minutes longer, until it is nicely browned. Unmold the shells onto a wire rack and cool.

For the pastry cream: Bring the milk to a boil in a saucepan. Meanwhile, whisk the egg yolk, sugar, vanilla, and cornstarch together in a bowl. Then whisk this mixture into the boiling milk and cook, stirring constantly, for 1 minute. Transfer to a bowl, cool to room temperature, cover, and refrigerate until just before serving time.

At serving time, fill the pastry shells with the pastry cream. Slice the banana and arrange the slices over the pastry cream in the tartlets. In a small bowl combine the apricot preserves and kirsch, and spoon the mixture over the bananas. Sprinkle the dates on top and serve.

Yield: 4 servings

Nutritional analysis per serving: calories 427; protein 5 gm.; carbohydrates 71 gm.; fat 14.1 gm.; saturated fat 7.2 gm.; cholesterol 85 mg.; sodium 40 mg.

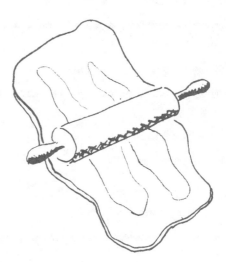

Crunchy Horns with Fruit

Molded cookies are the showpiece of this recipe. The soft cookie dough is literally brushed onto a very cold cookie sheet, so that it adheres on contact. This technique makes large, very thin cookies, which bake quickly. They can then be lifted off the sheet while still warm and pressed or formed into different shapes. If you allow the cookies to cool too long on the sheet, they get brittle and break as you try to mold them; should this occur, return them to the oven for a minute or so to soften them slightly before attempting to mold them again. ❦ I use dried as well as fresh fruit in the mix I serve with the cookies. Although this is a particularly nice combination of fruits, you can make substitutions based on your personal preferences and seasonal considerations.

For the cookies

¼ stick (2 tablespoons) unsalted butter, softened

¼ cup sugar

½ teaspoon pure vanilla extract

1 egg white

2 tablespoons all-purpose flour

For the fruit mix

8 ounces strawberries, washed, hulled, and cut into ½-inch pieces (1¾ cups)

4 dried figs, sliced thin (⅔ cup)

2 bananas (about ¾ pound), peeled and cut into ½-inch pieces

2 tablespoons lemon juice

2 tablespoons sugar

1 cup low-fat yogurt (optional)

1 teaspoon confectioner's sugar, for decoration

For the cookies: Preheat the oven to 400 degrees. Rub a nonstick cookie sheet with ½ teaspoon of the butter and place the sheet in the refrigerator. (If you have a particularly high-quality nonstick cookie sheet, you may omit the butter.) Place the remaining butter and the sugar in the bowl of a food processor and process for 15 seconds. Add the vanilla, egg white, and flour, and process for another 10 seconds.

Using a pastry brush, spread the cookie mixture onto the cold cookie sheet, forming it into 4 very thin round disks, each about 6 inches in diameter.

Bake the cookies at 400 degrees for 8 to 10 minutes, until nicely browned. Remove the sheet from the oven and lift the disks one at a time from the sheet with a metal spatula. Roll them while still hot around a metal cone to create a horn or press the cookies into ½-cup glass bowls to make "cups." Let the cookies cool, remove them carefully from their molds, and set them aside until serving time.

For the fruit mix: In a bowl, mix together the fruit, lemon juice, and 2 tablespoons sugar. Refrigerate until serving time.

At serving time, arrange the cookie horns on individual dessert plates with the open end of the horn in the center of each plate and the "tail" extending beyond the edge. Arrange the fruit mixture on the plates to create the illusion that it is spilling out of the horns. Alternatively, arrange the cookie cups on individual dessert plates and fill them with the fruit. Garnish with yogurt, if desired, spooning it on either side of the cookie horns or cups. Sprinkle the confectioner's sugar on the fruit, the cookies, and the plate. Serve.

Yield: 4 servings

Nutritional analysis per serving: calories 299; protein 3 gm.; carbohydrates 62 gm.; fat 6.6 gm.; saturated fat 3.8 gm.; cholesterol 16 mg.; sodium 21 mg.

Prickly Meringues with Fruit Sauce

I give these individual meringues a distinctive look by pulling up on the surface of the egg white mixture to create "prickly" points on top. ❦ Meringue used to be served more conventionally with a custard sauce made from cream and eggs. My intensely flavored fruit sauce, made from a puree of frozen raspberries that is mixed with preserves and combined with diced orange, is a delicious, more healthful alternative.

3 egg whites

½ cup sugar

1 teaspoon pure vanilla extract

For the fruit sauce

2 cups individually quick-frozen raspberries, thawed

⅓ cup seedless raspberry preserves

1 large seedless orange (about 10 ounces)

12 mint leaves, shredded

Preheat the oven to 200 degrees. Beat the egg whites until stiff but not dry. Add the sugar all at once and beat for about 10 seconds to incorporate it into the whites. Mix in the vanilla.

Using a spoon or a pastry bag fitted with a fluted tip, pipe four round or oval meringues onto a parchment-paper-lined tray. Using the end of the fluted tip, pull up on the surface of the meringues to create prickly points. Bake the meringues at 200 degrees for 3 hours. The meringues should be lightly browned and cooked throughout.

For the fruit sauce: Push the berries and preserves through a food mill fitted with a very fine screen. Some seeds may go through; if so, the mixture can be strained through a sieve, if desired. (You will have about 1 cup.)

Peel the orange so that the flesh is totally exposed and cut it into ½-inch pieces. (You should have about ¾ cup.) Combine with the raspberry mixture and the shredded mint.

To serve, spoon some of the sauce onto each of four dessert plates and place a meringue in the center of each plate. Serve immediately.

Yield: 4 servings

Nutritional analysis per serving: calories 243; protein 4 gm.; carbohydrates 59 gm.; fat 0.8 gm.; saturated fat 0.01 gm.; cholesterol 0 mg.; sodium 44 mg.

Guava Paste Toast with Mint

This dish holds happy taste memories of childhood for my wife. Her Puerto Rican mother served guava paste often, and I have learned to like it too, especially in combination with a little cream cheese and mint. You'll find it in the ethnic food sections of most super-markets and in Latin American specialty food stores. This is good not only as a dessert but also as an afternoon snack or buffet dish.

4 thin slices white bread, crusts removed

4 ounces cream cheese

1 can (1½ pounds) guava paste

24 mint leaves

No more than 30 minutes before serving, toast the bread slices lightly and cut each of them into six pieces. On each piece, place a small slice of cream cheese and top it with a small slice of guava paste. Garnish each toast with a mint leaf and arrange them on a plate. Serve as a dessert or snack.

Note: Leftover guava paste, well wrapped, will keep for several weeks in the refrigerator.

Yield: 4 servings

Nutritional analysis per serving: calories 308; protein 4 gm.; carbohydrates 48 gm.; fat 11.3 gm.; saturated fat 6.4 gm.; cholesterol 32 mg.; sodium 222 mg.

Apricot and Fig Soufflé

Flavored with a puree containing both dried apricots and apricot preserves, this soufflé has an intense taste that I like. Dried figs lend texture and provide interesting color contrast. ❦ The soufflé will puff nicely and can be served hot in the mold. It can also be made ahead and served cold as a kind of apricot pudding. As it cools, it will deflate, falling to about the level of the uncooked mixture in the mold. It is good either way on its own, or it can be served with yogurt or sour cream.

6 ounces dried apricots

¼ cup apricot preserves

⅓ cup diced (¼-inch dice) dried figs

½ teaspoon unsalted butter

5 large egg whites

1 tablespoon sugar

Confectioner's sugar (optional)

Yogurt or sour cream (optional)

Place the apricots in a saucepan with 1 cup water. Bring to a boil, cover, reduce the heat, and boil gently for 15 minutes. (All but about ⅓ cup of the water should have evaporated. If there is more, reduce it to this amount by boiling; if there is less, add enough water to make this amount.) Transfer the contents of the saucepan to the bowl of a food processor, add the preserves, and process until smooth.

Place the processed mixture in a bowl, fold in the figs, and set aside. (The recipe can be prepared to this point a few hours ahead.)

Preheat the oven to 375 degrees. Grease a 4-cup soufflé mold with the butter and set it aside.

About ½ hour before serving, beat the egg whites until stiff, add the sugar, and beat for a few more seconds to incorporate it. Gently fold and mix the apricot mixture into the egg whites and transfer the mixture to the buttered mold.

Bake the mold at 375 degrees for about 20 minutes, until the soufflé is puffy and barely set inside. Sprinkle with the confectioner's sugar, if desired, and serve immediately, as is or with a spoonful of yogurt or sour cream.

Yield: 4 servings

Nutritional analysis per serving: calories 234; protein 7 gm.; carbohydrates 54 gm.; fat 0.9 gm.; saturated fat 0.3 gm.; cholesterol 1 mg.; sodium 63 mg.

Café au Lait Granité

A s its name indicates, a *granité* is a somewhat coarse, granulated mixture. Not too sweet, it is sometimes served as a palate cleanser between courses at elaborate banquets. I serve it here as a light dessert. ❧ There are two equally good versions of this dish and I give them both here. In both, the frozen mixture is "shaved." This can be done with a hand grater, but it's easier to use a food processor fitted with a slicing blade.

1½ cups strong, good quality, brewed coffee

3 tablespoons sugar

2 tablespoons half-and-half

2 tablespoons half-and-half for garnish (optional)

4 strips lemon peel (optional)

2 tablespoons Kahlua (optional)

8 chocolate-coated coffee beans (optional)

Version 1
Mix the coffee, sugar, and half-and-half together in a bowl and then place the mixture in the freezer. Freeze until hard (at least overnight).

Defrost under refrigeration until the mixture resembles frozen slush and is soft enough to be scooped. If you are in a hurry, you can break the frozen block into a few pieces and process it in a food processor fitted with a slicing blade, pushing it through the feeding tube piece by piece. Return the "shaved" coffee mixture to the freezer until serving time. Spoon into demitasse cups.

Serving options (do any one or two of these):

- Spoon ½ tablespoon of half-and-half over each serving.

- Place a strip of lemon peel on top.

- Coat with ½ tablespoon of Kahlua.

- Add a couple of chocolate-coated coffee beans.

Version 2
Mix the coffee and sugar together in a bowl and freeze until hard (overnight).

Defrost under refrigeration until the mixture is soft enough to be scooped. If you are in a hurry, you can push the mixture through a food processor fitted with a slicing blade and then place the resulting "coffee snow" back in the freezer. Serve in demitasse cups with one or two of the serving options above.

Yield: 4 servings

Nutritional analysis per serving: calories 68; protein 0.5 gm.; carbohydrates 12 gm.; fat 2.0 gm.; saturated fat 1.4 gm.; cholesterol 8 mg.; sodium 5 mg.

Crêpes à la Confiture

As children, my brother and I would sit and watch my mother prepare crêpes and eat them as quickly as they came out of the pan—usually with homemade jam, but sometimes with just a sprinkling of sugar or a little grated chocolate. I duplicate this taste treat for my daughter for breakfast from time to time. It is easily done in a few minutes and is always a winner!

For the crêpes

⅔ cup all-purpose flour

2 large eggs

½ teaspoon sugar

¾ cup skim milk

1 tablespoon corn or canola oil

A little additional oil for greasing the skillet

For the fillings

- **The best quality jam or preserves: strawberry, apricot, quince, blackberry, plum, or the like**

- **Granulated sugar**

- **Grated chocolate**

Combine the flour, eggs, sugar, and ¼ cup of the milk in a bowl and mix with a whisk until smooth. (The mixture will be fairly thick.) Add the remaining milk and the tablespoon of oil and mix until smooth.

Lightly grease the bottom of an 8- or 9-inch nonstick skillet with a little oil and heat the pan over medium to high heat. When it is hot, add about 3 tablespoons of the crêpe batter and quickly tilt and move the skillet so the batter coats the entire bottom of the pan. (Move quickly, or the batter will set before the bottom of the skillet is coated and the crêpe will be thicker than desired.)

Cook for about 45 seconds on one side, and then turn and cook for about 20 seconds on the other side. As you make the crêpes, stack them on a plate, first-browned side down, so that when they are filled and folded this nicer side will be visible. The crêpes are best made and filled just before eating.

To fill, spread each crêpe with about 2 teaspoons of jam, or 1 teaspoon of sugar, or 2 teaspoons of grated chocolate. Fold in half, enclosing the filling, and then in half again. Eat immediately.

Yield: 4 servings (16 crêpes)

Nutritional analysis per serving: calories 314; protein 8 gm.; carbohydrates 44 gm.; fat 13.4 gm.; saturated fat 4.3 gm.; cholesterol 107 mg.; sodium 59 mg.

Jam Omelet Soufflé

T his is a simple soufflé, made with egg whites and a little egg yolk for color and flavor. Baked in an oval-shaped tray, it resembles a classic omelet. ❦ The egg mixture used here is the base, too, for the classic French *omelette norvégienne* or *omelette surprise*— what we in this country call baked Alaska. The traditional ice cream filling is replaced in my version with cake slices spread with fruit preserves and moistened with espresso coffee.

1 teaspoon unsalted butter

4 ounces pound cake, sponge cake, or cookies

¼ cup black currant (or other fruit) preserves

2 egg yolks

2 teaspoons pure vanilla extract

6 egg whites

½ cup sugar

¼ cup freshly brewed espresso coffee

1 teaspoon confectioner's sugar

Preheat the oven to 400 degrees. Grease an oval, stainless steel tray (about 12 inches long by 7 inches wide) with the butter. Cut the cake into ½-inch slices (if using cookies, leave them whole) and spread them with the preserves.

Mix the egg yolks lightly with the vanilla and set aside.

No more than an hour before cooking, beat the egg whites until firm. Add the granulated sugar in one stroke and mix for an additional 10 seconds, just long enough to incorporate the sugar. Using a large spatula, fold the egg yolk mixture into the egg whites. Place about one-fourth of the mixture on the buttered tray and spread it out so the entire length and most of the width of the tray is covered.

Arrange the cake slices in a single layer, preserves side down, on top of the egg mixture on the tray. Sprinkle the cake slices evenly with the espresso and then cover them with one-fourth of the remaining egg mixture, spreading and smoothing it with a spatula.

Place the remaining egg mixture in a pastry bag fitted with a star tube and use it to decorate the top and sides of the soufflé. Bake the tray at 400 degrees for about 15 minutes, until the surface of the soufflé is nicely browned and the mixture is just set inside.

Sprinkle with the confectioner's sugar and serve immediately.

Yield: 6 servings

Nutritional analysis per serving: calories 239; protein 6 gm.; carbohydrates 36 gm.; fat 7.9 gm.; saturated fat 2.3 gm.; cholesterol 100 mg.; sodium 80 mg.

Frozen Black Velvet

Kahlua, figs, and chocolate-coated coffee beans bring this simple dessert to a high level of sophistication. Served in crystal goblets, it makes a terrific finish for an elegant meal. Ice cream can, of course, be substituted for the yogurt if you are not counting calories. If you would rather not use alcohol, substitute a few drops of vanilla extract for the Kahlua.

1 pint good quality nonfat vanilla frozen yogurt

4 tablespoons Kahlua, or another coffee-flavored liqueur

4 dried figs, each cut into about 6 wedges

12 chocolate-coated coffee beans

Divide the frozen yogurt among four dishes and pour 1 tablespoon of the Kahlua over each serving. Arrange the fig wedges on top and around the yogurt, and sprinkle on the coffee beans. Serve.

Yield: 4 servings

Nutritional analysis per serving: calories 203; protein 3 gm.; carbohydrates 40 gm.; fat 1.1 gm.; saturated fat 0.5 gm.; cholesterol 1 mg.; sodium 50 mg.

Custard with Blueberry Sauce

This custard is quite lean; I use skim milk and a minimum of sugar. On its own, it might not be as rich-tasting as you would like, but in combination with a sauce of fresh blueberries, good quality apricot preserves, and cognac, it makes a beautiful dessert. ❦ The water bath surrounding the custard molds as they bake should not be allowed to boil or the custard will overcook. Remove the molds from the oven as soon as the custard is lightly set yet still somewhat jellylike if shaken. It will continue to firm as it cools.

For the custard

2 large eggs

¼ cup sugar

1 teaspoon pure vanilla extract

1¾ cups skim milk

For the blueberry sauce

¼ cup apricot preserves, best possible quality

2 tablespoons cognac

1 cup fresh blueberries

For the custard: Preheat the oven to 350 degrees. Break the eggs into a mixing bowl and beat them with a fork until they are well combined and there is no visible sign of egg white. Add the sugar, vanilla, and milk, and mix well to dissolve the sugar.

Arrange four small (¾ cup) soufflé molds in a roasting pan and strain the custard mixture into the molds. Surround the molds with enough lukewarm tap water to extend about three-quarters of the way up the sides of the molds.

Place the pan in the 350-degree oven and bake the molds for about 35 minutes, until the custard is barely set. Remove the molds from the water bath and cool them for at least 3 hours.

For the blueberry sauce: Mix the preserves and cognac together in a small bowl, adding 1 tablespoon water, if needed, to thin the preserves to the consistency of a sauce. Stir in the blueberries and set aside.

At serving time, unmold the custards on individual plates, spoon some blueberry sauce over and around them, and serve immediately.

Yield: 4 servings

Nutritional analysis per serving: calories 220; protein 7 gm.; carbohydrates 37 gm.; fat 2.8 gm.; saturated fat 0.9 gm.; cholesterol 108 mg.; sodium 92 mg.

Blueberry Crumble

This is an easy recipe that I prepare often in the summer, when berries are plentiful. I especially like it made with blueberries, but blackberries, boysenberries, and raspberries are good like this, flavored with a fruit preserve or jam, moistened with a little orange juice, and topped before baking with leftover cake or cookie crumbs. The crumble can be served on its own, with yogurt, or—if you want to splurge—with sour cream or whipped cream.

2 cups fresh or frozen blueberries (about 10 ounces)

¼ cup apricot preserves

2 tablespoons orange juice

3 ounces pound cake, sponge cake, or cookies, crumbled

1 cup yogurt

Preheat the oven to 375 degrees. Mix the blueberries, preserves, and orange juice together in a bowl and then transfer the mixture to a 3-cup gratin dish.

Crumble the cake or cookies on top, covering the blueberries entirely. Bake at 375 degrees for 30 minutes. Serve lukewarm, topped with 2 generous tablespoons of yogurt per person.

Yield: 4 servings

Nutritional analysis per serving: calories 234; protein 5 gm.; carbohydrates 39 gm; fat 7.4 gm.; saturated fat 2.2 gm.; cholesterol 35 mg.; sodium 70 mg.

Russian Cranberry Kissel

K*issel* is a classic Russian dessert that usually consists of a puree of acidic fruit. Any tart berries can be used, but cranberries are the classic choice. Sometimes the berries are merely combined with sugar and thickened with a little cornstarch. I add orange juice and rind to my version and serve the *kissel* with a little yogurt (if you want it richer, substitute sour cream) and garnishes of pomegranate seeds and mint.

1 package (12 ounces) fresh cranberries

1½ teaspoons grated orange rind

¾ cup orange juice

¼ cup sugar

1 teaspoon cornstarch

¼ cup plain yogurt or sour cream

2 tablespoons pomegranate seeds

A few sprigs of mint

4 cookies (optional)

Put the cranberries, orange rind and juice, sugar, and cornstarch in a stainless steel saucepan and bring the mixture to a boil over high heat, stirring occasionally. Cover, reduce the heat, and cook gently for approximately 10 minutes. The mixture will be thick and bright red. Set it aside to cool. (You should have about 2 cups.)

When it is cool, divide it among four glass goblets. Garnish with yogurt (or sour cream), a sprinkling of pomegranate seeds, and mint, and serve with cookies, if desired.

Yield: 4 servings

Nutritional analysis per serving: calories 128; protein 1 gm.; carbohydrates 31 gm.; fat 0.4 gm.; saturated fat 0.1 gm.; cholesterol 1 mg.; sodium 12 mg.

Grapefruit and Kiwi Ambrosia

This refreshing, satisfying dessert is the ideal finish for an elegant menu. The grapefruit is cut into membrane-free wedges and mixed with pieces of kiwi and sweet white sauternes-type wine. Intensely flavored sauternes, the greatest dessert wines in the world, are made from grapes attacked by the fungus *botrytis*, which shrivels them and concentrates their juice. This wine can also be served with the dessert.

2 Ruby Red grapefruits (1 pound each)

3 kiwis, peeled and cut into ½-inch pieces

½ cup sauternes-type sweet white wine

2 tablespoons Grand Marnier liqueur

8 Bing cherries

Peel the grapefruits with a sharp knife, removing all the skin and the underlying white pith so the flesh of the fruit is totally exposed. Cut between the membranes and remove the flesh in wedgelike pieces. Place the grapefruit pieces in a bowl and squeeze any remaining juice from the membranes over them before discarding the membranes.

Peel the kiwis and cut them into ½-inch pieces. Add them to the grapefruit along with the wine and Grand Marnier. Mix and allow to macerate for at least a few minutes and as long as a few hours before serving.

To serve, spoon the fruit into glass goblets or dessert dishes and top each serving with a couple of cherries.

Yield: 4 servings

Nutritional analysis per serving: calories 119; protein 1 gm.; carbohydrates 22 gm.; fat 0.5 gm.; saturated fat 0.03 gm.; cholesterol 0 mg.; sodium 4 mg.

Prunes and Grapefruit in Red Wine Sauce

T his combination of cooked prunes and raw grapefruit in a red wine sauce has an appealingly tart taste and is very pleasing to the eye, although one of the fruits could be eliminated and the other served on its own in this manner also. Either way, this simple fruit dessert is a welcome ending to a rich meal.

½ pound large pitted dried prunes (about 24)

2 tablespoons light brown sugar

¾ cup dry red wine

1 vanilla bean

¼ teaspoon black peppercorns

4 to 6 whole cloves

2 small Ruby Red grapefruits
(about 1½ pounds)

Place the prunes, sugar, red wine, and vanilla bean in a saucepan. Place the peppercorns and cloves on a small square of cheesecloth and tie them up together into a package (for easier removal after cooking). Add the cheesecloth package to the saucepan and bring the mixture to a boil. Cover, reduce the heat to low, and cook gently for 10 minutes.

Meanwhile, peel the grapefruits and, with a sharp knife, remove the segments from between the membranes so the grapefruit pieces are free of any thin surrounding "skin." Squeeze the membranes over a bowl to release any remaining juice. Add about ⅓ cup of the juice to the prunes in the saucepan and cool the mixture.

At serving time, remove and discard the cheesecloth package and divide the prunes among four plates. Arrange about 4 grapefruit segments alongside the prunes on each plate. Pour the prune cooking juices over the fruit and serve.

Yield: 4 servings

Nutritional analysis per serving: calories 220; protein 2 gm.; carbohydrates 50 gm.; fat 0.4 gm.; saturated fat 0.02 gm.; cholesterol 0 mg.; sodium 7 mg.

Grapes in Red Wine Sauce

This is a refreshing summer dessert that looks most attractive served in stemmed glasses. Yogurt gives the dish an appealing look, and its acidity contrasts nicely with the sweetness of the grapes and accompanying wine sauce. ❦ It is essential that you use Red Flame grapes here. They can withstand cooking better than most other grape varieties. Although their skins will crack, they won't fall apart the way many other grapes do when cooked.

1 cup sturdy, fruity red wine

1½ pounds seedless Red Flame grapes, removed from the stems and washed (4 cups)

¼ cup currant jelly

¼ teaspoon cinnamon

2 teaspoons potato starch

1 cup plain yogurt

Reserve 1 tablespoon of the wine. Place the grapes in a saucepan with the rest of the wine, the jelly, and the cinnamon. Bring to a boil, cover, reduce the heat, and boil gently for 4 to 5 minutes, just until the grapes begin to crack open.

Set the pan off the heat. Dissolve the potato starch in the reserved tablespoon of wine and stir into the grape mixture. Cool to room temperature and serve in stemmed glasses with a generous spoonful of yogurt.

Yield: 4 servings

Nutritional analysis per serving: calories 234; protein 4 gm.; carbohydrates 46 gm.; fat 1.4 gm.; saturated fat 0.7 gm.; cholesterol 3 mg.; sodium 49 mg.

Pears au Gratin

This is a nice way to use leftover French bread. Leftover cookies or cake can be substituted, in which case eliminate the butter and sugar. ❦ It is important that the pears be well ripened for this dish, even if this means buying fruit that is slightly damaged or has darkened skin; the skin will be removed and any remaining spots on the flesh of the sliced pears will be concealed under the crumbs of the topping. ❦ Sour cream or whipped heavy cream makes a nice addition, but the dish is very good without either garnish.

4 very ripe pears (about 1½ pounds), peeled, halved lengthwise, and cored

3 ounces day-old French-style bread

2 tablespoons unsalted butter

¼ cup sugar

½ cup pecan halves

Sour cream or whipped heavy cream (optional)

Preheat the oven to 375 degrees. Cut the pears lengthwise into ¼-inch slices, and arrange them in one slightly overlapping layer in the bottom of a 6-cup gratin dish.

Break the bread into the bowl of a food processor and process it until coarsely chopped. (You should have about 1¾ cups of coarse crumbs.) Add the butter, sugar, and pecans. Process until the mixture is mealy, and then sprinkle it evenly over the pears. Bake at 375 degrees for 30 minutes, until the topping is nicely browned. Allow to cool slightly.

Serve the pears lukewarm, with a little sour cream or heavy whipped cream, if desired.

Yield: 4 servings

Nutritional analysis per serving: calories 343; protein 4 gm.; carbohydrates 50 gm.; fat 16.1 gm.; saturated fat 4.5 gm.; cholesterol 16 mg.; sodium 124 mg.

Pears in Espresso

I like to use espresso in this recipe, but any leftover brewed coffee will do. I think that Bosc pears, which take longer to cook than most, lend themselves especially well to this preparation, although you can use another variety instead. If you can obtain tiny Seckel pears in your area, they are also good in this dessert. Pears are a good source of potassium and fiber.

4 Bosc pears (about 1½ pounds total), peeled and cored from the base with a small round scoop or a sharp-edged metal measuring teaspoon

2 cups espresso coffee

⅓ cup light brown sugar

1 teaspoon grated lemon rind

2 tablespoons Kahlua or another coffee-flavored liqueur

4 cookies (optional)

Stand the peeled and cored pears upright in a saucepan that will hold them snugly. Add the coffee and enough water (about 2 cups) to cover the pears completely; then add the sugar. Bring the coffee mixture to a boil, cover, reduce the heat to low, and boil gently until the pears are tender, 30 to 35 minutes.

Remove the pears from the liquid and arrange them in a serving bowl. Boil the liquid until it is reduced to 1 cup, stir in the lemon rind, and pour the mixture over the pears. Cool.

Add the Kahlua to the cooled dish and serve the pears cold, with cookies, if desired.

Yield: 4 servings

Nutritional analysis per serving: calories 183; protein 1 gm.; carbohydrates 44 gm.; fat 0.6 gm.; saturated fat 0.03 gm.; cholesterol 0 mg.; sodium 8 mg.

Pineapple Delice

The quality of this dessert depends entirely on the quality of the pineapple. If your pineapple is ripe and flavorful, this quick and easy preparation will be delicious; if it's not, the dessert is not worth making. ❦ Some people insist that, if you can pull out a leaf from the crown of a pineapple, the fruit is ripe. I think you should rely on your nose. A ripe pineapple will have pleasant, fruity smell.

½ teaspoon grated lime peel

1½ tablespoons lime juice

2 tablespoons honey

2 tablespoons kirsch (cherry brandy)

1 small ripe pineapple (about 2¼ pounds), leaves removed

4 slices pound cake or cookies (optional)

Mix the grated lime peel, lime juice, honey, and kirsch together in a large bowl.

Peel the pineapple, removing the skin and most of the black holes on the surface of the flesh. Stand the pineapple upright and begin cutting it vertically into ¼-inch slices, stopping when you get to the core, turning it 90 degrees, and cutting again, until the pineapple has been rotated 360 degrees on its base and all the flesh has been removed. Then, stack up the slices and cut them into 1½-inch-wide strips.

Add the pineapple strips to the bowl containing the other ingredients and mix well. Allow the pineapple to macerate in the lime juice mixture for at least 1 hour. Serve as is or with slices of pound cake or cookies.

Yield: 4 servings

Nutritional analysis per serving: calories 115; protein 1 gm.; carbohydrates 27 gm.; fat 0.5 gm.; saturated fat 0.03 gm.; cholesterol 0 mg.; sodium 2 mg.

Potted Plums with Phyllo Dough

I use plums here, but any fruit can be stewed in this way and finished with the dough on top. ❦ Phyllo dough is available packaged in the frozen food sections of most supermarkets. Conventionally, this thin dough is wrapped around fruit and the resulting packages baked. I find this process quite difficult—the dough tends to break, and then the fruit juices leak through or they make the dough soggy underneath. Instead, I gather one sheet of this tissuelike pastry into a loosely formed ball, perch it atop an individual serving of the fruit, and then bake the dish until this pastry "hat" is brown and crisp. It makes a beautiful presentation and is easy to do.

1 pound Santa Rosa plums (about 10)

2½ tablespoons unsalted butter

3 tablespoons shelled and skinned pistachio nuts

⅓ cup apricot preserves

**2⅓ tablespoons sugar
(1 tablespoon is optional)**

4 sheets phyllo (14 by 18 inches each), covered until ready to use (to prevent dryness)

Sour cream or whipped heavy cream (optional)

Preheat the oven to 350 degrees. Pit the plums and cut each into 4 wedges (8 cups total).

Heat 1½ teaspoons of the butter in a saucepan. When it is hot, sauté the plums with the pistachios, preserves, and 1 tablespoon water, covered, over high heat for 5 minutes, until the plums are soft. Remove the lid and cook 2 to 3 minutes longer to eliminate any moisture remaining in the pan. (The mixture should be thick, not watery.) Add up to 1 tablespoon of the sugar to the plums if they are too tart, and transfer them to a bowl.

Melt the remaining 2 tablespoons of butter. Unwrap the phyllo sheets, lay them out on a flat work surface, and, working quickly so the paper-thin pastry doesn't dry out, brush the top surface of the phyllo with the butter and sprinkle it with the remaining 4 teaspoons of sugar.

Place ½ to ⅔ cup of the plum mixture in each of four small (1 cup) ramekins. Fold each sheet of phyllo in half, butter side out, and gather it gently into a loose tissuelike ball, taking care not to squeeze it. Place one ball of the phyllo on top of each ramekin and arrange the ramekins on a tray. Bake at 350 degrees for 25 to 30 minutes.

Serve lukewarm, with sour cream or whipped cream, if desired.

Yield: 4 servings

Nutritional analysis per serving: calories 308; protein 4 gm.; carbohydrates 51 gm.; fat 10.9 gm.; saturated fat 4.9 gm.; cholesterol 19 mg.; sodium 89 mg.

Strawberries in the Sun

I t takes about three consecutive sunny days to "cook" these berries. If an extended period of sun is not a sure thing where you live, you may cook them instead in a 175- to 180-degree oven for up to 20 hours, the total time depending on how much liquid you want around the berries and how thick you like it to be. You want a fairly heavy syrup, but remember that it will thicken substantially as it cools. If you intend to serve the berries as a sauce for ice cream or as a topping for another dessert, you will want more syrup and a slightly thinner consistency than if you intend to eat the berries as a jam on bread. ❦ This recipe produces whole berries that are almost candied in the syrup. Remember that, in a conventional strawberry jam, the amount of sugar is almost equal in weight to the strawberries. In this recipe, half as much sugar by weight is used. ❦ For the syrup, sugar and water are cooked together on top of the stove and then the berries are added. The mixture is neither stirred nor cooked very long on top of the stove, so the berries remain whole. Then the mixture is placed in a roasting pan, covered with a screen (to repel insects) and placed in the sun. The liquid evaporates slowly and the berries swell in the syrup.

1½ pounds (3¼ cups) sugar (more if berries are not ripe)

1½ cups water

3 pounds (1½ quarts) small, ripe strawberries, hulled and washed

Toast or cookies (optional)

Combine the sugar and water in a large stainless steel saucepan. Bring the mixture to a boil and boil for 6 to 8 minutes, until the mixture reaches the soft-ball stage (240 degrees). Add the berries, cover, and cook in the syrup for about 2 minutes. Shake the pan gently (instead of stirring) and set the pan aside, covered, off the heat for about 10 minutes. At this point, the berries will have rendered their liquid and be very limp.

Transfer the mixture to a roasting pan. (The berry mixture should be about ¾ to 1 inch thick in the pan.) Cover the pan with a window screen and place it in direct sun for 2 to 3 days, until the syrup is reduced to the desired thickness. If sun is not available, place the pan in a 175- to 180-degree oven for 15 to 20 hours, until the syrup is of the desired thickness. Pour the mixture into jars and refrigerate until ready to use.

To serve, spoon 3 to 4 tablespoons of the preserves per serving into small dessert dishes and serve as is or with a piece of toast or a cookie, if desired.

Yield: 6 to 8 servings (three 12-ounce jars)

Nutritional analysis per serving: calories 376; protein 1 gm.; carbohydrates 96 gm.; fat 0.6 gm.; saturated fat 0.03 gm.; cholesterol 0 mg.; sodium 2 mg.

Glazed Strawberries

T his stunningly beautiful recipe is best made when large, ripe, full-flavored berries—preferably with stems—are available. The berries are dipped in warm currant jelly, which hardens around them as it cools. If the glazed berries are to stand for a long time on a buffet table, you might want to add a little unflavored gelatin to the jelly to make it even more binding and resistant to melting.

12 large strawberries with stems

1 jar (10 ounces) currant jelly

A few sprigs basil or edible flowers or herbs, for garnish

4 or 8 cookies (optional)

Chill a plate in the refrigerator. Wash the berries and dry them thoroughly with paper towels.

Place the currant jelly in a saucepan and warm it over low heat until it has melted and is smooth.

Holding the berries by their stems, dip them, one at a time, in the currant jelly. When they are thoroughly coated with the jelly, lift the berries out and drain off any excess jelly by scraping the berries gently against the rim of the pan.

Place the glazed berries on the very cold plate and refrigerate them until serving time.

At serving time, arrange three berries on each plate and decorate with the basil, flowers, or herbs. Serve with cookies, if desired.

Yield: 4 servings

Nutritional analysis per serving: calories 113; protein 0.4 gm.; carbohydrates 29 gm.; fat 0.2 gm.; saturated fat 0.01 gm.; cholesterol 0 mg. sodium 7 mg.

When we join with

friends and family on

holidays and

special occasions,

we sometimes don't count

calories—we indulge.

At other times we are

more careful.

MISCELLANEOUS

Basic Chicken Stock, page 158

Curried Oil, page 159

Cilantro Oil, page 160

Bouquet Garni, page 161

Herbes de Provence, page 162

Ficelles, page 163

Basic Chicken Stock

S tock is used throughout this book in soups, sauces, stews, and other recipes. It takes very little work to make your own stock; mostly it is a matter of staying home for the several hours it takes to cook. ❦ Chicken backs and necks are now available packaged at most supermarkets. If you don't see them, ask a butcher there to package some for you, or buy turkey backs, necks, and gizzards instead. From a health standpoint, it is well worth making your own stock, since it will be practically fat-free and salt-free. A flavorful money saver, it can be frozen in small quantities and used as needed.

3 pounds chicken bones (necks, backs, and gizzards, skinless or with as little skin as possible)

6 quarts lukewarm tap water

1 tablespoon Herbes de Provence (see page 162)

1 large onion (about 8 ounces), peeled and cut into four pieces

12 whole cloves

4 bay leaves

1 tablespoon dark soy sauce

Place the bones and water in a large stockpot and bring to a boil over high heat. Reduce the heat and boil gently for 30 minutes. Most of the fat and impurities will rise to the surface during this time; skim off as much of them as you can and discard them.

Add the remainder of the ingredients, return the liquid to a boil, and boil gently for $2\frac{1}{2}$ hours. Strain it through a fine-mesh strainer or a colander lined with a dampened kitchen towel or paper towels.

Allow the stock to cool. Then, remove the surface fat and freeze the stock in plastic containers with tight lids.

Yield: 3 quarts (12 cups)

Nutritional analysis per one-cup serving: calories 37; protein 2 gm.; carbohydrates 3 gm.; fat 1.6 gm.; saturated fat 0.4 gm.; cholesterol 0 mg.; sodium 164 mg.

Curried Oil

lavoring oils is a new technique that young chefs use widely today. It is used by many restaurants to add flavor and color to their dishes, and it is relatively easy to do. This flavored oil will keep in the refrigerator for about a month. A beautiful color, it can be used to flavor vinaigrettes, soups, or stews, and it is also good for sautéing fish.

½ cup corn oil

1 teaspoon curry powder

Place the oil and curry powder in a jar, cover with a tight lid, and shake well. Set aside at room temperature for at least 12 hours and as long as 2 days, shaking the jar a few times during this period.

At the end of the maceration period, pour the clear oil into another receptacle and discard the curry powder mixture that remains in the bottom of the jar. Use the oil as needed.

Yield: ½ cup

Nutritional analysis per one-tablespoon serving: calories 121; protein 0.03 gm.; carbohydrates 0.2 gm.; fat 13.7 gm.; saturated fat 1.7 gm.; cholesterol 0 mg.; sodium 0.1 mg.

Cilantro Oil

I use cilantro to flavor this oil, but if the assertive flavor of this herb is not to your liking, you can substitute parsley, chives, or your own favorite mixture of fresh green herbs. ❦ Shaken well before each use, the flavored oil can be used as is and will keep, refrigerated, for three or four days. Or you can strain out the herbs and then remove and reserve the oil that rises to the top of the remaining liquid. In this form, the oil will keep for at least a week in the refrigerator and can be used as needed. Either variation is good; combined with vinegar and seasonings, the unstrained version makes an especially appealing vinaigrette dressing.

1 bunch (4 ounces) cilantro with stems

⅓ cup water

½ cup corn, peanut, or canola oil

Process the cilantro with the water in a mini-chop until pureed. Transfer the puree to a saucepan, bring it to a boil, and immediately set the pan off the heat. When the puree has cooled, pour it into a jar with a tight lid, add the oil, cover, and shake well. Allow to sit for at least 2 hours to develop flavor. Use as is.

For a more refined variation, after the 2-hour macerating period, pour the mixture into a bowl lined with a clean kitchen towel and press it through the towel into the bowl. Set the liquid aside for 30 to 45 minutes, and then skim off the green oily residue from the top of the mixture and discard it. Pour out and reserve the green oil in the middle, but discard the watery liquid in the bottom of the bowl. Use the green oil as needed.

Yield: about ½ cup strained

Nutritional analysis per one-tablespoon serving: calories 122; protein 0.2 gm.; carbohydrates 0.2 gm.; fat 13.7 gm.; saturated fat 1.7 gm.; cholesterol 0 mg.; sodium 2 mg.

Bouquet Garni

A French bouquet garni is a mixture of aromatic herbs used as a flavoring for stocks, stews, and casseroles. Traditionally, these herbs are tied together in a small bunch with kitchen twine and submerged in the cooking vessel. At the end of the cooking period—or when the herbs have imparted sufficient flavor to the dish—they are easily removed and discarded. ❦ The classic bouquet garni is made of parsley stems (the leaves are chopped for other uses), sprigs of thyme, and bay laurel leaves. Often, however, greens of leek, a rib of celery, a carrot, and sprigs of available herbs such as tarragon, rosemary, and savory are added.

Required herbs

15 to 20 parsley stems

A few sprigs thyme

2 or 3 bay laurel leaves

Optional herbs and vegetables

A few sprigs tarragon, rosemary, and/or savory

Greens from 2 leeks

1 rib celery

1 carrot

Bundle the herbs and vegetables together and tie them securely or, if you are using thyme leaves or pieces of bay leaves too small to secure with twine, wrap the mixture in a cheesecloth package before adding it to the pot.

Herbes de Provence

Herbes de Provence is a blend of dried herbs that is used frequently in the cooking of southern France. This blend always contains thyme, savory, marjoram, and oregano in equal proportions, but lesser amounts of other herbs can also be included. *Herbes de Provence* is, of course, readily available commercially in Provence and elsewhere in the Mediterranean basin, and it can be purchased in many specialty food stores here. It is similar to Italian seasoning, which can be found in most American supermarkets and is a good substitute. ❦ In response to numerous requests from "Today's Gourmet" viewers who have been unable to find *herbes de Provence* in their area, I have devised a recipe for a homemade version of this aromatic herb blend made with fresh herbs that you dry yourself. If fresh herbs aren't available at all or only some of those listed below are available, you can make your *herbes de Provence* mixture by combining commercially produced dried herbs in the proportions indicated below.

Required herbs

Thyme

Savory

Marjoram

Oregano

Optional herbs

Sage

Rosemary

Lavender flowers

Fennel seeds

For the required herbs: Dry the leaves of fresh thyme, savory, marjoram, and oregano by arranging them (one herb variety at a time) in one layer on one or more cookie sheets and placing them in a low oven (180 degrees) until dry (12 to 20 minutes, depending on the herbs), or air dry them outdoors in the summer shade. Mix together equal amounts of these dried herbs.

For the optional herbs: Dry the sage and rosemary leaves and the lavender flowers as indicated above. Mix together equal proportions of these herbs with a like amount of fennel seeds.

Then, following a 2-to-1 formula, mix a whole portion of the required herbs mixture with a half portion of the optional herbs mixture. Enclose in plastic bags, sealing them tightly to preserve the freshness of the herbs. Use in recipes as needed.

Ficelles

"String" Breads

Ficelles, or "string" breads, are traditional in French cooking. My recipe includes wheat bran and coarse bulgur wheat, which gives the loaves an earthy, chewy texture. As its name implies, the bread is shaped into very thin string- or ropelike strips. It cooks much faster in this form and has a wonderfully crunchy crust. ❦ You can recrisp loaves you have made ahead by running them under cold water briefly and then returning them to a 425-degree oven for about 10 minutes. You can also partially cook the loaves initially, baking them for only about 10 minutes—until they reach their maximum size but are still pale in color and not yet crisp. In this form, they can be refrigerated or frozen. When you are ready to complete the baking and browning of the thawed or frozen loaves, place them in a preheated 425-degree oven for 12 to 15 minutes.

1 envelope (2 teaspoons) granulated yeast

¼ teaspoon sugar

2½ cups all-purpose flour (about 13 ounces)

⅓ cup wheat bran

2 tablespoons bulgur wheat (preferably the coarse variety available in health food stores)

¾ teaspoon salt

½ teaspoon canola oil

2 tablespoons coarse cornmeal

Place 1 cup tepid water in the bowl of a food processor and sprinkle the yeast and sugar over it. Mix a few seconds, just long enough to combine the ingredients, and then let the mixture sit to "proof" for 5 minutes. It should be foamy and have a yeasty smell.

Add the flour, bran, bulgur, and salt, and process for about 45 seconds. The mixture will form a soft ball.

Grease a mixing bowl with the canola oil and place the ball of dough in the bowl, turning it once to coat it on both sides with the oil. Cover the bowl with plastic wrap and let the dough rise in a warm, draft-free place for about 45 minutes, until it is puffy and about triple in size. "Break" the proofed dough by gently pulling it from the sides of the bowl and pushing it down into the center.

Transfer the dough to a cookie sheet and extend it by alternately rolling and squeezing it until you form it into a cylinder about 16 inches long. Cut the cylinder lengthwise into four equal very thin strips of dough.

Sprinkle the cornmeal on the cookie sheet and roll the *ficelles* in it. Then arrange them on the sheet with enough space between so they have room to rise. Cover with plastic wrap and let rise for about 30 minutes.

Place a small cake pan on the bottom shelf of the oven and preheat the oven to 425 degrees.

When the *ficelles* have risen, cut several gashes about 1/4 inch deep in the tops of them or snip them on top with scissors, creating a design to your liking.

Place the *ficelles* on the middle shelf of the oven and throw a few ice cubes in the hot cake pan underneath to create steam (which helps make the exterior of the bread crustier). Bake for about 20 minutes, until the loaves are brown and crisp. Cool on a rack and serve lukewarm or at room temperature.

Yield: 4 servings

Nutritional analysis per serving: calories 388; protein 12 gm.; carbohydrates 81 gm.; fat 1.8 gm.; saturated fat 0.2 gm.; cholesterol 0 mg.; sodium 416 mg.

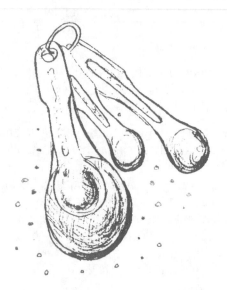

The concerns of modern,

well-educated eaters

go beyond how food tastes

and how it is presented.

The quality of the products

in our diet directly

affects the quality of our

health and the health of our

families.

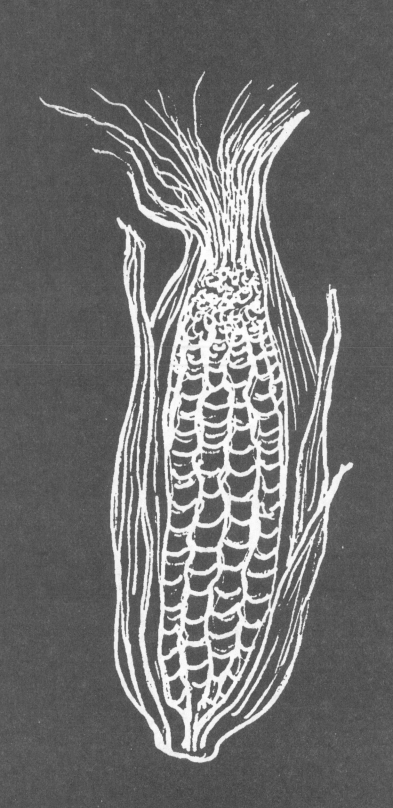

HEALTH NOTES

To me, modern cuisine is really common sense cuisine. Today's menus should consist of foods that are tasty and beautiful, as well as a variety of foods that help to maintain healthy weight. Meals should be low in fat, saturated fat, and cholesterol, contain plenty of vegetables, fruits, and grain products, and include sugars, salt, and alcohol in moderation.

TECHNIQUES AND EQUIPMENT

I have found that using certain techniques and equipment in the kitchen can enhance the nutritional value of foods. For instance, fats are the most calorie-laden food that we eat. With few exceptions, any techniques and equipment that reduce our fat intake will improve our diet.

One excellent way to cut down on fats in cooking is to use nonstick pans. The amount of fat used to sauté in a nonstick pan is less than half of what might be used in an untreated pan. I like to use nonstick pans with a permanent finish when I sauté and fry.

Grilling is another great way to enhance the flavor of foods without adding fat or sodium. There is great diversity in the types of grills available today. When I grill, I like to use natural wood chips such as apple wood, olive wood, or cherry wood for their delicious smoky flavor and ability to produce high heat. I often use wood charcoal because it is pre-cooked so it turns to hot coal more quickly. Charcoal briquettes are petroleum based and should be reduced to a gray ash color before you cook over them. This reduces the tar flavor that food can pick up from them.

VITAMINS AND MINERALS

For years we have been concerned about the amounts of vitamins and minerals in our diets. Modern cooking has given us some new insight into this old subject.

We now know that the old way of cooking vegetables, which was to blanch them in large pots of boiling water and then refresh them in cold water before seasoning, resulted in the loss of essential vitamins and minerals. I recommend cooking vegetables in a small amount of boiling water just until the water disappears, thus retaining maximum amounts of vitamins and minerals.

Iron intake is a particular concern for many people, especially women. Many of my recipes, such as Christmas Oysters (page 58), Puerto Rican Pork and Beans (page 92), and Seafood with "Handkerchiefs" (page 76) are high in iron.

PROTEIN

Red meat, long maligned as a high-fat protein source, has moved into the nineties as a much lighter main course item. Now that steers and pigs are being raised to produce leaner meat, we can get our iron and protein from these red meat sources without worrying about fat intake. When we trim the meat properly before cooking and serve smaller portions, red meat is part of a healthy gourmet diet. For example, my recipes for Steak *Maître d'Hôtel* (page 103) and Slow-Cooked Pork Roast (page 94) are high in protein and low in calories and fat.

FIBER

Today, experts recommend a diet high in fiber to help reduce cholesterol. For you and me, that means approximately 25 to 30 mg. of fiber per day. Luckily, water-soluble dietary fiber is contained in some delicious packages. Fiber is a part of plant foods. It is found in abundance in whole-grain breads and cereals, fresh and dried fruits, and vegetables. My menus all include these foods. Some recipes especially high in fiber are Broccoli with Butter (page 109), Vegetable Burgers (page 117), and Lamb Shanks and Beans Mulligan (page 95).

COMPLEX CARBOHYDRATES

Complex carbohydrates, which give us long lasting energy by slowly converting to sugars during digestion, do not necessarily need to be combined with high-fat foods to be delicious. Complex carbohydrates are found in many of the foods that also happen to be rich in fiber, vitamins, and minerals, such as whole grain breads, cereals, pastas, rice, beans, and potatoes.

GRAINS

Adding whole grains to your diet is a great way to add protein, fiber, and complex carbohydrates. I often use traditional grains such as grits in nontraditional ways. My Tomatoes Stuffed with Yellow Grits (page 51) is a good example. Also I recommend using grains that are now gaining in popularity, such as bulgur, featured with roasted Cornish hens on page 88.

CALORIES

Reducing calories does not necessarily mean eating tiny portions of trendy food. There are many hearty, filling dishes that are very low in calories. Some of these dishes in *Today's Gourmet II* are: Fillet of Pork *Charcutière* (page 93), Breast of Veal *Cocotte* (page 102), Chicken in Coriander Sauce (page 83), and Red Snapper in *Brunoise* Sauce (page 81).

I have suggested several dessert recipes that are quite low in calories, too. While a typical portion of dessert often contains as many as 500 calories per serving, the following desserts are much lighter and contain under 130 calories: Russian Cranberry *Kissel* (page 145), *Café au Lait Granité* (page 139), and Glazed Strawberries (page 154).

On special occasions, we tend to consume a few more calories than we would during the rest of the year. I have suggested a Sunday gathering menu that is delicious but contains approximately half the calories of a typical feast. The menu features Dried and Fresh Mushroom Soup (page 19), *Poulet Rôti* (page 86), *Coquillettes au Gruyère* (page 122), and *Crêpes à la Confiture* (page 140).

CHOLESTEROL

The American Heart Association recommends that we consume no more than 300 mg. of cholesterol per day. In most instances, I use oils instead of butter to cut down on cholesterol. In addition, my recipes minimize the number of egg yolks per serving, since yolks are high in cholesterol.

FATS AND LOW-FAT ALTERNATIVES

Experts believe that a healthy diet is one in which no more than 30 percent of the daily calories consumed are derived from the intake of fat. To achieve this percentage, I sometimes substitute low-fat alternatives in my recipes. For example, I may use nonfat or low-fat yogurt instead of sour cream.

Some fats have proved beneficial to health. Salmon, although it is a fatty fish, contains what is now described by experts as "heart-healthy fats" or omega 3s. These omega 3s help keep blood from getting "sticky" and forming clots that lead to heart attacks. Eating fatty fishes has also been correlated with lower levels of fats (called triglycerides) in the blood . Because of these benefits, health experts are urging us to eat more fish, up to 15 pounds per year.

OILS

Today's supermarket offers a vast selection of oils. It is important to understand the nature of oils to know which one to choose. For instance, some oils are lower in saturated fat than others, some are more strongly flavored, and some may burn at a relatively low temperature, giving off bad odors and flavor.

At room temperature, all oils are liquid fat. Some oils, such as palm and coconut oil, are very high in saturated fat and therefore can boost the level of blood cholesterol. In much of my cooking, I use the oil that is lowest in saturated fat—canola oil.

Extra virgin olive oil is usually dark, with a rich olive flavor. The color and flavor are the result of olive solids present in the oil. Extra virgin olive oil is so named because it has been removed from the olives by mechanical pressing, from the sheer weight of the olives. No heat or chemical processes are used to extract this oil. The olive solids, which impart flavor and color, burn at fairly low temperatures, so extra virgin olive oil is best used for salads and marinades.

The best oils to use in sautéing are flavorless safflower and canola oils, or, for mild flavor, peanut oil. They are ideal for sautéing because they can withstand high temperatures without burning.

SUGARS

It is important to use moderation when consuming refined sugar. Refined sugar can lead to tooth decay and, when combined with fat, can be tremendously caloric. But who can resist sweet treats on special occasions? For this reason, I have included recipes for *Pain au Chocolat* and *Noisettes* (page 131) and Banana Tartlets (page 132). A small bit of a rich dessert can help you to feel satisfied without overdoing it.

SALT

I have some special tips for cutting down on salt. Because I like highly seasoned foods, I use a variety of seasonings as salt substitutes. Tabasco sauce, plenty of fresh herbs, and strong-flavored spices are excellent substitutes.

The key to reducing the amount of salt used in cooking is to bring out the natural flavor in the food itself. For example, if you crystallize the juices on the outside of meat by browning it well first, as I do in my Fricassee of Veal recipe (page 100), you can bring up the flavor without adding an excess of salt. Another way to enhance flavor is to use citrus fruit, such as lemon or orange, or the numerous fresh herbs and spices available today. And don't forget about flavor-enhancing cooking techniques such as grilling, steaming, and broiling.

VEGETABLES

Vegetables are the most important kind of food to emphasize in our diets. They are naturally low in calories and high in fiber, vitamins, and minerals. Whenever possible, I buy organic fruits and vegetables for their fantastic flavor and guaranteed wholesomeness. My friend Alice Waters, of Chez Panisse restaurant, says that by purchasing organic fruits and vegetables we support the people who work to preserve and enhance our farmlands.

When I was young, my mother was an organic gardener, and she didn't even know it! But this was in a time when growing food without chemicals was a way of life, not a specialty.

INDEX

Page numbers in *italic* designate the location of the menu that includes the indexed dish; those in sans serif designate the location of the photograph of the recipe.

A

Achiote (annatto) seeds, in yellow rice with orange rind, 124

Allspice (Jamaican peppercorns), in tuna steaks with peppercorns, 82

Anchovies, in cauliflower *gribiche*, 45

Apple:
  cheese, apple, and nut mélange, *5*, 23, 130
  tart, country, *4*, 128–29

Apricot and fig soufflé, *6*, 138

Artichoke bottoms, lobster in, *11*, 29, 78–79

Asparagus, ragout of, *2*, 108

Aspic:
  clarified, 52–53
  eggs in, with tarragon, *9*, 52–53

B

Banana tartlets, *11*, 132–33

Bass, striped, *nage courte* of, *14*, 56

Beans:
  mulligan, lamb shanks and, *32*, 95
  Puerto Rican pork and, *12*, 92

Beef:
  daube of, in red wine, *6*, 35, 104–105
  steak *maître d'hôtel* (with parsley butter), *3*, 103
  stock for Hanoi soup, 20–21

Beets, with skate and flavored oil, 64–65

Beurre maître d'hôtel, 103

Bitochki (ground meat patties), veal, 99

Black Velvet, frozen, *3*, 38, 142

Blueberry:
  crumble, *2*, 144
  sauce, custard with, 36, 143

Blue cheese, in cheese, apple, and nut mélange, *5*, 23, 130

Bouquet garni, 161

Bread:
  ficelles ("string" breads), 163–64
  pain au chocolat and *noisettes*, *5*, 23, 131
  and tomato, gratin of, *9*, 34, 116

Brie cheese, in eggplant and red pepper terrine, 25, 46–47

Broccoli with butter, *11*, 29, 109

Broth, lobster, with pasta, 18

Brown rice, wehani, 125

Brunoise sauce, red snapper in, 28, 81

Bulgur wheat:
  in *ficelles* ("string" breads), 163–64
  pilaf, *8*, 123
  stuffing for Cornish hens, 31, 88–89

C

Cabbage, savoy:
  Oriental savoy salad, *11*, 119
  sausage, potato, and cabbage soup, *4*, 41

Calories, 168

Canola oil, low in saturated fat, 169

Caper sauce, for grilled veal chops, 34, 101

Carbohydrates, complex, 168

Cauliflower *gribiche*, *7*, 45

Cèpe mushrooms, in soup, 19

Chicken:
 breasts, stuffed "Kiev-style," *8*, **33**, 84–85
 in coriander sauce, *9*, 83
 roasted (*poulet rôti*), *14*, 86–87
 stock, 158
Cholesterol, 169
Cilantro (coriander):
 chicken in coriander sauce, 83
 oil, 160
 in Puerto Rican pork and beans, 92
 in scallop seviche, 27, 67
Codfish in olive and horse-radish sauce, *9*, **26**, 57
Coffee:
 in *café au lait granité*, 139
 espresso, in jam omelet soufflé, 141
 espresso, pears in, 150
 liqueur, in frozen Black Velvet, **38**, 142
Coquillettes au Gruyère (pasta shells with swiss cheese), *14*, 86–87, 122
Coriander sauce, chicken in, 83
Cornish hens, stuffed and roasted, *7*, **31**, 88–89

Couscous of lamb, *10*, 96–97
Cranberry *kissel*, Russian, *9*, **38**, 145
Crêpes à la confiture, *14*, **37**, 140
Crunchy horns (molded cookies) with fruit, *13*, 134–35
Cucumber with tarragon, *10*, **28**, 110
Curried oil, 159
Custard with blueberry sauce, *13*, **36**, 143

D
Daikon radish, with grilled salmon fillets, 80
Daube of beef in red wine, *6*, **35**, 104–105

E
Eggplant:
 grilled, on greens, *8*, 48
 and red pepper terrine, *10*, **25**, 46–47
Egg roll wrappers:
 and fennel and pear salad, 43
 in seafood with "hand-kerchiefs," **26**, 76–77
Eggs:
 in aspic with tarragon, *9*, 52–53
 fines herbes omelet, 75
 prickly meringues with fruit sauce, 136

Endive with olives, *11*, 49
Escarole, in salad with *saucisson*, 44
Espresso:
 in jam omelet soufflé, 141
 pears in, *14*, 150

F
Fats, 167, 169
Fennel and pear salad, *12*, 43
Fiber, 168
Ficelles ("string" breads), 163–64
 pain au chocolat and *noisettes*, **23**, 131
Fig and apricot soufflé, *6*, 138
Fines herbes omelet, *5*, 75
Fish, *see* Seafood; specific varieties of fish
Fricadelles (patties), turkey, with vegetable sauce, *4*, 90–91
Fricassee of veal, *13*, 100
Fruit mix, with crunchy horns, 134–35
Fruit sauce, with prickly meringues, 136

G

Ginger, in beef stock for Hanoi soup, 20–21

Gnocchi *maison*, *12*, **33**, 120–21

Grains, 168

Granité, café au lait, *12*, 139

Grapefruit:

and kiwi ambrosia, *4*, **38**, 146

and prunes in red wine sauce, *8*, 147

Grapes in red wine sauce, *7*, 148

Greens:

for clarified aspic, 52–53

composed salad, 42

with cured salmon in molasses, **30**, 61

grilled eggplant on, 48

Gribiche, cauliflower, *7*, 45

Grilling, 167

Grits, white, in vegetable burgers, 117

Grits, yellow, tomatoes stuffed with, *5*, 51

Gruyère, coquillettes au (pasta shells with swiss cheese), 122

Guava paste toast with mint, *12*, 137

H

Ham:

and peas, stew of, *3*, 112

spinach, ham, and parmesan soufflé, *2*, 54–55

Harissa (hot pepper sauce), 96–97

Hazelnuts, in *pain au chocolat* and *noisettes*, **23**, 131

Herbs:

bouquet garni, 161

herbes de Provence, 162

in omelet (*fines herbes*), 75

Hijiki seaweed, with Christmas oysters, 58–59

Horseradish and olive sauce, codfish in, **26**, 57

Horseradish-yogurt sauce, for veal *bitochki*, 99

I

Iron, 167

J

Jalapeño pepper, in scallop seviche, **27**, 67

Jam (preserves):

crêpes à la confiture, **37**, 140

omelet soufflé, *10*, 141

K

Kissel, Russian cranberry, *9*, **38**, 145

Kiwi and grapefruit ambrosia, *4*, **38**, 146

L

Lamb:

couscous of, *10*, 96–97

leg of, roasted, *6*, **32**, 98

shanks and beans mulligan, *7*, **32**, 95

Linguini, in red pepper pasta with walnuts, 72–73

Lobster:

in artichoke bottoms, *11*, **29**, 78–79

broth with pasta, 18

M

Menus, 1–15

"Autumn Fare," 7

"A Budget Feast," 3

"City Fish and Country Fowl," 7

"Classic and Modern Mix," 9

"Cold Weather Comfort," 6

"Corner Café Food," 12

"Elegant and Modern," 8

"Foods of the Forest," 4

"French Atlantic Cooking," 11

"From Garden and Grill," 2

"From the North Sea to North Africa," 10

"A Make-Ahead Menu," 2

"A Melting Pot Menu," 13

"Menu for a Sunday Gathering," 14
"Midweek Dinner—a Family Meal," 4
"A Pépin Potpourri," 13
"Personal Favorites," 5
"Provençal Tastes," 10
"Puerto Rican Connection," 12
"Russian Flavors," 9
"Special Guest Menu," 14
"Summer Elegance," 6
"Thrifty Kitchen," 3
"Today's Approach to Old Classics," 8
"Vegetable Feast," 5
"Vietnamese Flavors," 11
Meringues, prickly, with fruit sauce, 8, 136
Minerals, 167
Molasses, cured salmon in, 30, 60–61
Mushroom(s):
    Portobello, grilled, 2, 111
    puree, stuffed in chicken breasts, 84–85
    soup, hot or cold, 14, 19
    in tomatoes stuffed with yellow grits, 51
    wild, with toast, 4, 50
Mustard sauce, for scallops in scallion nests, 28, 66

N

Nage courte of striped bass, 14, 56
Noisettes, pain au chocolat and, 23, 131
Nonstick pans, 167
Nori (seaweed sheets), salmon in, 30, 62
Nuoc mam (Vietnamese fish sauce):
    with Hanoi soup, 20–21, 24
    in squid salad à la Binh, 68

O

Oeufs en gelée (eggs in aspic), 52–53
Oeufs mollets (soft-boiled eggs), 52–53
Oil, flavored, 159, 160
    steak with beets and, 64–65
Oils, 169
Olive(s):
    endive with, 11, 49
    and horseradish sauce, codfish in, 26, 57
Olive oil, extra virgin, 169
Omelet:
    fines herbes, 5, 75
    jam, soufflé, 10, 141
Onion:
    in potatoes boulangère, 114
    soup gratinée, 40
    soup with vermicelli, 12, 40
Orange rind, with yellow rice, 124

Oxtail, in beef stock for Hanoi soup, 20–21, 24
Oysters:
    Christmas, 8, 58–59
    in seafood with "handkerchiefs," 26, 76–77

P

Pain au chocolat and noisettes, 5, 23, 131
Parmesan cheese, in spinach, ham, and parmesan soufflé, 2, 54–55
Parsley butter, for steak maître d'hôtel, 103
Pasta:
    lobster broth with, 18
    onion soup with vermicelli, 40
    red pepper, with walnuts, 4, 72–73
    shells with swiss cheese, 122
Pastina, in lobster broth with pasta, 18
Pastry cream, for banana tartlets, 132–33
Pea pod soup, 3, 22
Pear(s):
    in espresso, 14, 150
    and fennel salad, 12, 43
    au gratin, 11, 49

Peas and ham, stew of, *3*, 112

Pecans:
  caramelized, in composed salad, 42
  cheese, apple, and nut mélange, *23*, 130

Pepper, red:
  and eggplant terrine, *10*, 25, 46–47
  pasta with walnuts, *4*, 72–73
  sauce, for Christmas oysters, 58–59

Peppercorns, tuna steaks with, 82

Peppers, hot Thai, in squid salad à la Binh, 68

Peppers, jalapeño, in scallop seviche, *27*, 67

Phyllo dough, potted plums with, *36*, 152

Pilaf, bulgur wheat, *8*, 123

Pineapple *delice*, *9*, 151

Plums, potted, with phyllo dough, *3*, *36*, 152

Pork:
  and beans, Puerto Rican, *12*, 92
  fillet of, *charcutière*, *12*, *33*, 93
  roast, slow-cooked, *3*, 94

Portobello mushrooms, grilled, *2*, 111

Potato(es):
  boulangère (sliced and baked), *6*, 114
  Darphin (shredded and sautéed), *3*, 113

  in gnocchi *maison*, *12*, *33*, 120–21
  sausage, potato, and cabbage soup, *4*, 41
  sauté *à cru*, *5*, 115
  sautéed, 113, 115
  in watercress soup, 39

Poulet rôti, *14*, 86–87

Protein, 167

Prunes and grapefruit in red wine sauce, *8*, 147

R

Red meat, and fat, 167

Red pepper:
  and eggplant terrine, *10*, 25, 46–47
  pasta with walnuts, *4*, 72–73
  sauce, for Christmas oysters, 58–59

Red snapper in *brunoise* sauce, *10*, *28*, 81

Red wine sauce:
  grapes in, 148
  prunes and grapefruit in, 147

Rice:
  risotto with vegetables, 74
  wehani brown, *13*, 125
  yellow, with orange rind, *12*, 124

Risotto with vegetables, *5*, 74

S

Salad:
  composed, *6*, 42
  with cured salmon in molasses, 61
  fennel and pear, *12*, 43
  Oriental savoy, *11*, 119
  with *saucisson*, *5*, 44
  squid, à la Binh, *13*, 68

Salmon:
  cured, in molasses, *10*, *30*, 60–61
  fillets, grilled, *2*, 80
  in *nori* (seaweed sheets), *7*, *30*, 62
  in seafood with "handkerchiefs," *26*, 76–77

Salt, reducing, 170

Sauce:
  blueberry, custard with, *36*, 143
  brunoise, red snapper in, *28*, 81
  caper, grilled veal chops with, *34*, 101
  coriander, chicken in, 83
  for fillet of pork *charcutière*, 93
  fruit, prickly meringues with, 136
  harissa, for couscous of lamb, 96–97
  horseradish-yogurt, for veal *bitochki*, 99

Sauce (*continued*):

lemon and vinegar, for salmon in *nori*, 30, 62

olive and horseradish, codfish in, 26, 57

red pepper, for Christmas oysters, 58–59

red pepper, for pasta with walnuts, 72–73

red wine, grapes in, 148

red wine, prunes and grape fruit in, 147

vegetable, turkey *fric-adelles* with, 90–91

Saucisson with salad, 5, 44

Sausage, potato, and cabbage soup, 4, 41

Sautéing, oils for, 169

Sauternes, in grapefruit and kiwi ambrosia, 38, 146

Savoy cabbage:

Oriental savoy salad, *11*, 119

sausage, potato, and cabbage soup, 4, 41

Scallions:

with scallops, 28, 66

in tomatoes stuffed with yellow grits, 51

Scallop(s):

in scallion nests, *6*, 28, 66

in seafood with "handkerchiefs," 26, 76–77

seviche, *13*, 27, 67

Seafood:

bass, striped, *nage courte* of, *14*, 56

codfish in olive and horse-radish sauce, *9*, 26, 57

with "handkerchiefs," *8*, 26, 76–77

lobster broth with pasta, 18

lobster in artichoke bottoms, *11*, 29, 78–79

oysters, Christmas, *8*, 58–59

red snapper in *brunoise* sauce, *10*, 28, 81

salmon, cured, in molasses, *10*, 30, 60–61

salmon, grilled, *2*, 80

salmon in *nori*, *7*, 30, 62

scallop seviche, *13*, 27, 67

scallops in scallion nests, *6*, 28, 66

skate with beets and flavored oil, *2*, 64–65

squid, grilled, on water-cress, *3*, 27, 69

squid salad à la Binh, *13*, 68

tuna steaks with pepper-corns, *9*, 82

Seviche, scallop, *13*, 27, 67

Shallots:

in beef stock for Hanoi soup, 20–21, 24

wild mushroom toast, 50

Shellfish, *see* Seafood; specific varieties of shellfish

Skate with beets and flavored oil, *2*, 64–65

Snapper, red, in *brunoise* sauce, *10*, 28, 81

Soufflé:

apricot and fig, *6*, 138

jam omelet, *10*, 141

spinach, ham, and parmesan, *2*, 54–55

Soup:

Hanoi, *11*, 20–21, 24

onion, with vermicelli, *12*, 40

pea pod, *3*, 22

sausage, potato, and cabbage, *4*, 41

watercress, 39

Spinach:

with Christmas oysters, 58–59

spinach, ham, and parmesan soufflé, *2*, 54–55

Squid:

grilled, on watercress, *3*, 27, 69

salad à la Binh, *13*, 68

Star anise, in beef stock for Hanoi soup, 20–21, 24

Stew:

couscous of lamb, *10*, 96–97

daube of beef in red wine, *6*, 35, 104–105

lamb shanks and beans mulligan, *7*, 32, 95

peas and ham, *3*, 112

Strawberries:

glazed, *6*, 154

in the sun, *2*, 153

Sugars, 170

Swiss cheese, pasta shells with, 122

T

Tarragon:

cucumber with, 28, 110

eggs in aspic with, 52–53

Tart, country apple, *4*, 128–29

Tartlets, banana, *11*, 132–33

Techniques and equipment, 167

Terrine, eggplant and red pepper, *10*, 25, 46–47

Toast:

guava paste, with mint, *12*, 137

wild mushroom, *4*, 50

Tomato(es):

and bread, gratin of, *9*, 34, 116

sauce, raw, 46–47

stuffed with yellow grits, *5*, 51

Tuna steaks with peppercorns, *9*, 82

Turkey *fricadelles* with vegetable sauce, *4*, 90–91

V

Veal:

bitochki (ground meat patties), *13*, 99

breast of, *cocotte*, *2*, 102

chops, grilled, with caper sauce, *14*, 34, 101

fricassee of, *13*, 100

Vegetable(s):

burgers (patties), *14*, 117

cooking of, 167

daube of beef in red wine, 35, 104–105

in diet, 170

risotto with, 74

sauce, turkey *fricadelles* with, 90–91

Vermicelli (angel hair pasta), onion soup with, 40

Vinaigrette, garlic-Dijon, for salad with *saucisson*, 44

Vinaigrette, sherry:

for composed salad, 42

for fennel and pear salad, 43

Vitamins, 167

W

Walnuts, red pepper pasta with, 72–73

Watercress:

grilled squid on, 27, 69

in seafood with "handkerchiefs," 26, 76–77

soup, hot or cold, 39

Wehani brown rice, *13*, 125

Wine, red:

daube of beef in, 35, 104–105

sauce, grapes in, 148

sauce, prunes and grapefruit in, 147

Y

Yogurt, frozen, in frozen Black Velvet, 38, 142

Yogurt-horseradish sauce, for veal *bitochki*, 99

Z

Zucchini julienne, *9*, 118

Today's Gourmet with Jacques Pépin
Season Two

The best meals, like the best television shows, are born out of collaboration, and "Today's Gourmet" is no exception. Generous donations of time, food, furnishings, equipment, and wine brought together Jacques's marvelous menus in such a way that KQED could then present his artistry in the kitchen to public television viewers all over the country. Peter Koehler, Diane Green, and Chef Jan Birnbaum at San Francisco's Campton Place Hotel Kempinski gave Jacques a true home away from home while he was taping the series. Steve Goldstein and Jill Novack at Levi Strauss & Co. responded rapidly and generously to our request for wardrobe. Our food purveyors, wineries and wine distributors, and cookware and appliance manufacturers all made it possible for KQED to present Jacques's recipes in the style they deserve. This was ensconced in as lovely a homelike setting as we could imagine, thanks to the generosity of the companies and retail stores that provided the dishware, linens, and furniture seen on our studio set. Contributions such as these are the backbone of public television production. This was all made complete by the generosity of Molly Chappellet, the Marin County Farmers Market, and the monks and students at the Green Gulch Farm Zen Center, who provided us with locations where we taped the introductions to each episode. The beautiful flowers and produce you see at the beginning of each show are products of the love and care these gardeners lavish upon their land, and we're grateful to them for sharing their beautiful spaces with us. ❦ A profound thank you—from the bottom of our hearts, and the bottom of our stomachs—to all who provided us with production assistance and support.

Peggy Lee Scott, *Producer*

Peter L. Stein, *Executive Producer*

WINES PROVIDED BY:
Associated Wine Distributors
Bordeaux Wine Bureau
Buena Vista Winery
Clicquot Inc.
Dreyfus-Ashby, Inc.
Fetzer Vineyards
The Hess Collection
Kermit Lynch Wine Merchant
Le Monjea Distingue Wine
    Importers
Merryvale Vineyards
Murphy-Goode Estate Winery
Paterno Imports
Seagram Chateau & Estate
    Wines Co.
William Grant & Sons, Inc.

FOOD PROVIDED BY:
Allied SYSCO
California Crayfish
California Meat
C. J. Olson Cherries
East Coast Exotics, Inc.
Marin County Farmers Market
Modesto Foods
Rapelli of California

SPECIAL THANKS:

CAMPTON PLACE HOTEL
Kempinski San Francisco

Levi Strauss & Co.
Ames Gallery
Angray Flowers
Bernardaud
Bourgeat USA
Chantal Cookware

Chappellet Vineyards Garden
Crate&Barrel
D. Porthault & Co.
Farberware, Inc.
General Electric Appliances
George V Collection
Isgro & Co.
Iwatani International Corp.
La Parisienne Posters
Le Creuset of America
Macy's California
Oscartielle Equipment Co.
Pak-Sher Quicksheets
Pierre Deux
Pottery Barn
Safeway, Inc.
Thermador
Trade Associates Group Ltd.
Williams-Sonoma
Zen Center at Green Gulch

NOTES